THE BOOK OF MARY

Adoration of the Magi. Flemish, Circa 1525.

THE BOOK OF

MARY

BY HENRI DANIEL-ROPS

Translated from the French by

ALASTAIR GUINAN

HAWTHORN BOOKS, INC., *Publishers*

NEW YORK

First Edition, March, 1960

NIHIL OBSTAT
DANIEL V. FLYNN, J.C.D.
CENSOR LIBRORUM

IMPRIMATUR
✠ FRANCIS CARDINAL SPELLMAN
ARCHBISHOP OF NEW YORK

JANUARY 1960

The nihil obstat and imprimatur are official declarations that a book or pamphlet is free of doctrinal or moral error. No implication is contained therein that those who have granted the nihil obstat and imprimatur agree with the contents, opinions or statements expressed.

CONTENTS

CONTENTS

[6]

ILLUSTRATIONS

Frontispiece: *Adoration of the Magi,* Flemish, Circa 1525.

The Annunciation, attributed to Jan van Eyck, 1385-1441.

Head of the Virgin, Bernardino Luini, 1475?-1533?.

The Visitation, Domenico Ghirlandaio, 1449-1494.

The Nativity, Bernardino Luini, 1475?-1533?.

Adoration of the Shepherds (detail), Giorgione, 1478-1510.

Adoration of the Magi (Altar Wings), by the Master of Darmstadt Passion.

The Flight into Egypt, Giotto, 1266-1336.

The Presentation in the Temple, Benjamin West, 1738-1820.

Christ Among the Doctors, Carl Bloch, 1834-1890.

Miracle at Cana, François le Fond, 1850?-1900?.

The Descent from the Cross, Rembrandt van Rijn, 1606-1669.

Assumption of the Virgin, Bartolomé Murillo, 1618-1682.

The illustrations appear in this order between pages 128 and 129.

[7]

PART I

The Quest for Our Lady, Mary

ONE

THE QUEST

A FEW PARAGRAPHS at the beginnings of the narratives of Saint Luke and Saint Matthew, some passing allusions incidental to the account of Our Lord's public life, and finally, a dark figure drawn in silhouette by Saint John in his description of the drama of Calvary—these are the basis of our knowledge of one who, apart from Jesus himself, is the most appealing of all the figures of whom we read in the Gospels. When, therefore, we compare the great role which the Virgin Mary nowadays exerts in Christian devotional thought, when we consider the *Theotokos* of Daphne and Mt. Athos reigning in glory over the Byzantine Church, when we think of Our Lady hovering over the faithful of the western world as patroness of such cathedrals as Amiens, Reims, and Chartres in France, and as the Mediatrix to whom prayer is raised at Lourdes, at La Salette, at Fatima—how enormously disproportionate, in the light of the textual foundation upon which it rests, must seem the majestic forms of that universal devotion to Mary which we today behold. Mary, Mother of Christ, is but guardedly revealed to us by the inspired books; yet she is the best known personage in them, save Christ alone, and there is none other, beside him, who appeals to so many hearts.

Herein lies a fact of great historic significance, one which is indeed linked to the basis of our civilization. It is undeniable that the Blessed Virgin occupies a place beyond parallel in the devotional life of millions of souls, for the prayer to her which we call the *Angelical Salutation* is, doubtless, more frequently repeated, by reason of its occurrence in the Rosary, than even the *Lord's Prayer,* the "Our Father," which is addressed to God himself. It is undeniable that the literature of Europe, from its earliest stages, has taken her, as it continues to take her, as a subject to so great an extent that a mere Marian bibliography would fill volumes. It is undeniable that the art of seventeen or eighteen hundred years has tirelessly renewed forms under which men express their love of Mary. All these facts are beyond refutation. It seems as if those few brief and unexpanded allusions in the Gospel contain within themselves the ability to develop abundantly, just as does that mustard seed which is described as the smallest of all seeds but is nevertheless destined to grow into a great tree to which come the birds of the air that they may build their nests.

It is interesting to investigate the base on which all these developments have been erected. There are many good Christians who are but slightly familiar with the Holy Scriptures and who scarcely make any distinction between the varied elements on which rests their devotion to Our Lady. Some of these elements are clearly found in Scripture, others spring from traditions which are very old and are worthy of deep respect even though no canonical text supports them. There are still other elements which we often owe to the interpreters of beautiful artistic concepts, but which have only a spirit of pious devotion to commend them to us. Finally, there are elements which distinctly reveal that great power of the development of dogma which the Church throughout the centuries has, with infallible certainty, employed so that she may enter ever more deeply into the meaning of the revelation which God has made to man. There is no doubt that the same impulse of faith underlies a Catholic's belief in the virginity of Mary, his celebration of the charming feast of her Presentation, and his firm adhesion to the dogma of her Immaculate Conception. Nevertheless, the historic foundation of these three concepts is not identical; and it is quite legitimate to draw distinctions.

Is Mary an historical person? There is no more doubt of that than that Christ himself is. What we are to investigate are the circumstances and conditions of her historic existence.

TWO

MARY IN THE GOSPELS

LET US RE-OPEN THE GOSPEL to seek the figure of Mary.[1] The most delightful picture of Mary fixed in our hearts is that which so many artists have given us when, as by an illumination of supernatural light, we see the amazed young maiden "full of Grace" whom the angel greets, the maiden who murmurs her acceptance of the Divine Will. But one of the four evangelists, Saint Luke, that sensitive portrayer of women, saints or penitents—he whom Dante has called "the herald of indulgence"—has described this scene. It is to Saint Luke that we owe our knowledge of "the tidings brought to Mary," of that angelical greeting which faithful lips repeat tirelessly in prayer. It is to him that we owe the record of that simple dialogue, ringing with conviction, when the Virgin is at first astonished by a promise which runs counter to Nature's law, but then, from the depth of her ever-faithful heart, expresses her complete submission to the will of God. It is Saint Luke, too, who, as if to establish this further, tells us of Mary's visit

[1] The Gospel texts which refer to Mary will be found in Part II of this book.

[14]

to her cousin Elizabeth to whom the Lord had also done great things, and who was even then carrying the future Baptist, Saint John. Their meeting furnished the occasion to give us another prayer in that wondrous song of joy in God which we have in the *Magnificat*. Here, if we are to proceed chronologically, we must put aside the third Evangelist and refer to the text of the first. Saint Luke had been satisfied to tell us merely that the Virgin Mary was "espoused to a man named Joseph, of the House of David." With what delicacy of touch does Saint Matthew supply details of the reaction of this man before the mystery which he saw being accomplished in the womb of his young betrothed, and of the assurances by which the Lord, through the voice of his angel, quieted the perplexity which arose in Joseph's heart. So it is that Matthew tells us in two lines that, being thus reassured "Joseph took her as his spouse," and that "although he had not known her, she gave birth to a son, whom he called Jesus." On this great event, the Nativity, it is Saint Luke who has more to say; and we must, therefore, return to his Gospel.

Once more, the third evangelist is now our only guide. Had his text been lost, we would not know the history of the census ordered by Rome which obliged Joseph and Mary to leave the little Galilean village of Nazareth in order to go to Bethlehem, in Judea, that they might there be entered on the official registers. Without Saint Luke we would not be able to picture to ourselves the lowly couple vainly seeking a place in some overcrowded inn and finally finding refuge in a stable, where Mary brought the Child into the world, wrapped him in swaddling clothes and laid him in a manger. Without Saint Luke we would know nothing of the angelic choir singing in the Palestinian night as they gave tidings to a few wonder-struck shepherds of the coming of the Saviour.

[15]

Nor would we have any inkling of that touching scene of the newborn Child being presented in the Temple while he was surrounded on all sides by prophetic foretellings of a glory and a sorrow strangely to be intermingled in his life.

Saint Luke then goes on to suggest very briefly the boyhood of Jesus when he tells us that *he advanced in wisdom and age and grace before God and men* (II; 52). Yet, for some details about the threshold of this childhood life and for a kind of foreshadowing of glory to come, it is to Saint Matthew that we must look in his account of an important episode. It is Matthew who shows us the visit of the Magi, and the restless figure of Herod, the ruler of Palestine. Matthew then tells of the massacre of the Innocents and of the flight into Egypt when Mary and Joseph carried the Child with them. Saint Matthew follows Saint Luke in his account of the return to Nazareth after the angel's warning.

From the time that she brings her child back to their home village, it may be said that Mary recedes, little by little, into the background. We find, however, the incident of the Temple which took place during the boyhood of Jesus. The Child dallied there, and his worried parents found him discoursing with the Doctors. From this time, we begin to perceive that mysterious gap which now shows itself and which is to become more manifest between Christ and his Mother. "How is it that ye sought me? Knew ye not that I must needs be in my Father's house?" This episode, of which it is Saint Luke (II; 49) alone who tells us, is quite in accord with what is to be perceived, henceforth, in the demeanor of Jesus in regard to her from whom he had taken his human flesh.

The public life of Christ now begins. What place does Mary have in it? The answer must be that it is a place singularly small. We may sense her presence not far from him even when she is not to be seen in the crowd which surrounds him. She plays no outstanding part. On but one occasion does the Gospel show her in the forefront, and this is at the time of the Marriage at Cana, an event recorded, again, by only one of the Evangelists. That this Evangelist should be Saint John is a fact worthy of note, for the recounting of miracles is not of frequent occurrence in the text of the Fourth Gospel.[2] Yet, although Mary at Cana is shown to us quite realistically and in a way expressive of her complete faith in Jesus, the reply which she received from him raises problems in itself. Indeed, it may even be said to be a disturbing reply. From henceforth there is but little trace of her. Two brief allusions seem to indicate a voluntary separation of Jesus from his Mother as if to say that in order to fulfill his mission he must break every tie. The three Synoptics each record one of these: *Who is my Mother?* and *Who are my brethren?* (Mark III; 33, Matt. XII; 46, Luke VIII; 19). Luke, alone, reepats for us the second allusion (Luke XI; 27). Mary's face is lost among the throng of the first followers of Our Lord. There is no way in which we can discern her.

It is not until the final moment that we see her again. The touching figure that we now behold is no longer that of the young girl who shines forth from the opening lines of Saint Luke and Saint Matthew. She is now the Sorrowful Mother standing at the foot of the Cross of whom the Sequence *Stabat Mater Dolorosa* sings. It is she Saint John shows us standing beside her Son in his agony, it is she whom, by a last bequest, Jesus confides to the care of his beloved disciple. After this we find but a word in the Acts of the Apostles, and from it we learn that as Mary had been present at the Crucifixion, she was also present to receive the miraculous

---

[2] Only seven miracles are recorded in this Gospel.

honor of the Holy Spirit's descent on the day of Pentecost, and is thus to be associated with the definitive founding of the Church. Concerning Mary, the Mother of Christ, nothing more is known from the canonical sources.

THREE

THE TESTIMONY OF THE TEXTS

How are we best to estimate the value of those pages of the Gospel in which are supplied almost our only basis—certainly our most trustworthy basis—for knowledge of Our Lady? A degree of difficulty may, first of all, be felt in the fact that of the incidents to which we have referred, incidents which, if put together, might supply an outline for *a life of Mary*, a report of each is given by only one Gospel writer.[1] Although the chief events which make up the biography of Our Lord are known to us on the threefold testimony of the Synoptics, (frequently confirmed, as well, by Saint John), the Annunciation, the Visitation, the Nativity, and the Presentation of Our Lord in the Temple, the Marriage at Cana, and the presence of Mary on Mount Calvary rest on the testimony of but one witness. The only two facts of major significance of which we possess evidence from more than one document are that Mary, a Virgin, conceived by the Holy Spirit, and that her spouse,

[1] It is true that an exception to this statement must be made in respect to the allusion to the Mother of Jesus which we have already cited from the three Synoptics; but the allusion actually gives us no information about Mary herself.

who was to become the foster father of Jesus, was Joseph. Saint Luke and Saint Matthew affirm both these details.

Nevertheless, that further information about Mary is supplied to us by only one of the Evangelists does not actually constitute a serious problem. That it should be Saint John alone reporting the presence of Mary at the foot of the Cross can be readily explained; for it may well be that in their terror the majority of the disciples of Our Lord had fled and did not dare witness the death of their Master. It is suggested by the Synoptics and stated according to very old traditions that they had gone to hide themselves among the tombs in the lower part of the City. It was Saint John, the well-beloved of Jesus, who alone had the fortitude to remain with him. And it is from John himself that the information supplied by the Fourth Gospel comes.

In the incident of the Marriage at Cana the part taken by Mary, although important, is not actually the leading role. As we have seen, only Saint John records it. It may properly be observed that the Fourth Evangelist, who wrote forty or forty-five years after the others,[2] obviously tried not to repeat the preceding accounts which were already being publicly read throughout the Church. Saint John's aim was rather to complete them. So it is that the basic elements in his text are often exclusively his own; and, as he was the favored disciple, and the disciple most intimately associated with his Master, this is only to be expected. He had, for example, a special right to record the dialogue between Jesus and the Samaritan woman, that with Nicodemus, and also the instruction con-

[2] We may recall that Saint Matthew wrote his Gospel in Aramaic between 50 and 55 A.D. and that it was translated into Greek about 63; that Saint Mark wrote his about 55-62, and Saint Luke his about 63, while the Fourth Gospel should not be dated earlier than sometime toward the close of John's life, between 96 and 104.

cerning "the bread of life" (John VI, 41 and following) despite the fact that other very important facts furnished by the Synoptics find no place in his Gospel. An example is the narrative of the Institution of the Eucharist. The incident at Cana is one of his additions, and like every element which Saint John decided to add, it has a particular kind of symbolism about it: it follows the line of thought of what Clemens Alexandrinus has termed "the Gospel eminently spiritual."

However, as far as concerns the early chapters of Luke and Matthew which make up "the Gospel of the Nativity," the question may seem more embarrassing. How much reliance should we place upon these passages which constitute a seemingly fortuitous addition to the basic Gospel?

To begin with we may say that every reader who is animated by good faith must acknowledge the tone of profound conviction which marks both narratives. There is more than one way of reporting an event, and it is easy enough for a writer to indicate that he does not quite believe what he is saying, without expressing it openly. So it is that Livy readily allows it to be understood that he does not take the fable of Romulus and Remus seriously; while Herodotus conveys as much about the more or less miraculous birth of Cyrus the Great. On the other hand, Matthew and Luke unreservedly subscribe to the truth of what they report.

An analysis of the style forbids the thought that the passages in the first and third Gospels which refer to Mary can be from the hands of authors other than those who wrote the rest of these works. The opening passages are identical in language with the remaining portions of these Gospels and are entirely homogeneous with them. In the latter parts of the Gospel of Saint Luke, one finds the same note of delicacy and the refined sense of psychology and poetry characteristic of the opening passages, while in the first chapter of Matthew it is easy to discern those Aramaicisms and Hebraicisms of one who is often called "the Christian Rabbi."

The most ancient manuscripts of the New Testament known to us contain the opening passages of Matthew and Luke as integral parts. These are the *Codex Sinaiticus,* which dates from the fourth century and is now in the British Museum, and the *Codex Vaticanus,* also of the fourth century, whose beautiful uncial script in three columns makes it a prized item in the Vatican Library.

Moreover, it is to be remarked that the earliest among the Church Fathers, the first of the major heresiarchs, and even the pagans themselves, refer to these passages of the Gospels just as they do to the rest of these books. Saint Ignatius of Antioch, who was martyred in 107, declares that Jesus was "truly born of a Virgin" and he says: "The Prince of this world knows not the virginity of Mary nor the birth and death of the Lord: these much discussed mysteries were done in God's secret way." Saint Justin, the great second century writer, follows, step by step, Saint Luke's account of the Annunciation. Saint Irenæus, bishop of Lyon, who died about 203, is responsible for that great concept so beloved of the Middle Ages which sees Mary as the new Eve. He presents the idea in these terms: "Humanity, destined for death by one virgin, was saved by another virgin," and he bases his remarks on Saint Luke. Cerinthus and Carpocrates, both heresiarchs, refer to Saint Matthew; and Marcion, who upset Rome about 135 by propagating his doctrine denying the humanity of Jesus, expressed his distaste for the manger, the swaddling clothes, and all the circumstances surrounding the birth of Our Lord. Celsus the Pagan, known as the Voltaire of the

[22]

second century, mocked at all that Saint Matthew tells us of the visit of the Magi, of the Massacre of the Holy Innocents, and of the flight into Egypt. It is entirely certain that at the end of the first century, or at the beginning of the second, the opening chapters of Matthew and Luke were regarded as integral parts of the Gospels.

The inevitable conclusion is that these chapters are documents which have exactly the same degree of value as the rest of the text. However, they did not form part of the primitive religious instruction or the traditional body of doctrine which the small company of the Apostles commonly held: they do contain details added by the two Evangelists for personal reasons, and they are certainly based on special sources of knowledge.

As far as Saint Luke is concerned, it may be that his source was the very best that could be found—Mary herself. Twice during his account of the birth and the childhood of Christ he feels it necessary to tell us: "Mary stored up all these things in her heart" (Luke II; 19 and 51). It is well known that according to a charming tradition of the Church of Jerusalem, Saint Luke is considered as having been the first to paint a portrait of the Madonna. Saint Thomas Aquinas accepted this tradition, and in the fourteenth century Nicephorus Calixtus cited, in support of it, the testimony of the ecclesiastical historian Theodore the Lector (circa 530). According to this writer, the Empress Eudoxia, while on a pilgrimage, sent this portrait to her sister-in-law, Pulcheria, the wife of the Emperor Theodosius II. However, despite the attractive charm which surrounds it, this tradition of Saint Luke as the portrait painter of Mary is unsupported by history; and as Père Lagrange [3] has put it, it may be no more

[3] See Bibliography.

[23]

than "the expression of another tradition which the text itself suggests in showing the care taken by this Evangelist to gather together all information bearing upon the Mother of Jesus."

All that we know of Saint Luke tends to support this interpretation. The cultivated physician, an intelligent man who accompanied Saint Paul on his missionary journeys, was undoubtedly of an inquiring and observant temperament. He shows a most remarkable psychological sense, especially in matters of feminine psychology. When he paints the two sisters of Lazarus, Martha so busy and Mary, who preferred to listen, or the pardoned sinner, how they spring to life under his pen! He shows his inquiring mind, his zest for information: it is he alone who names among the holy women, Joan, the wife of Chuza, who was steward of the tetrarch Herod, from whom he certainly received some information. There is nothing surprising in the notion that he may have questioned the Mother of Christ. It is more than probable that during the three years of the captivity of his chief, Saint Paul, in Palestine, he had time to talk to witnesses and to take notes. What is more natural than that he should have made use of the result of these investigations?

When he was writing his Gospel, Luke, an Hellenized Jew of Asia Minor, addressed himself particularly to the pagans. His insistence on showing Jesus as the Saviour of all men establishes this, as well as the minute detail he gives about Palestine. This would not have been necessary had he been writing for a Jewish audience but it is quite normal in a pupil of the Apostle of the Gentiles. As a matter of fact Saint Luke, in writing for pagans, must have been animated by a very special motive.

Père Lagrange has pointed out that since the Oriental sovereigns who had been deified were considered to be Saviours, it had been thought necessary to attribute marvelous characteristics to their births as a testimony to their divine nature. In the year 238 B.C., the birthday anniversary of Ptolemy was observed as a special feast, as the inauguration of a time of joy for mankind. About the first century before Christ, the sacred manifestation or epiphany of Antiochus of Commagene was celebrated in Asia Minor. And, in the year 9 of the Christian era, one of the Asian proconsuls had proposed that the birthday of the "divine Caesar," Augustus, be taken as the beginning of the civil year, inasmuch as it evidently had marked the commencement of an era of wondrous events and of the regeneration of human kind. In being careful to vindicate the title of *Saviour* for a Child as lowly as the Saviour Christ, one so little regarded that only a stable screened his birth, did not Saint Luke act under the influence of evident design, a design whose purpose was to call a halt to the false glory of this world? The first Christians were able to go straight to the point of Christ's message as it is expressed in the body of the Gospels; but to the same degree that veneration of Jesus increased and the circumstances of his childhood began to attract the interest of men, there would be a lessened opposition to setting those circumstances in contrast to the legends of the pseudo-Saviours, the divinized rulers of the Orient; for the circumstances were themselves extraordinary and wonderful.

Saint Matthew's intentions certainly cannot have been identical with those of Saint Luke. He was a Jew who wrote within a Jewish frame of reference. The Gospel text reveals him to us as a publican, a minor Jewish official of the customs and tax service. Saint Irenæus tells us: "It was among the Hebrews and in the Hebrew language that Matthew gave his Gospel to the world." Nowadays it is generally agreed that

[25]

the original text of Matthew's Gospel was Aramaic. Moreover, there are certain details in his work which serve to establish the fact that he was addressing himself to the Jews. For example, he alludes to the tiniest letter of the Hebrew alphabet (V; 18), or to the craft employed to pervert the meaning of the Law (XXIII).

Now at Jerusalem, among the Jews, the point of view which agitated those who listened to the preaching of the Apostles certainly turned on the Messianic mission of Jesus. Was he a descendant of David? Was it truly at Bethlehem that he had been born? Had the prophecies actually been fulfilled in him? It was Matthew's desire to prove to the Jews that Jesus was truly the One awaited, the One who could fulfill in himself all the prophetic texts of Scripture. At the very beginning of his Gospel, the genealogical information which he gives casts into relief the Davidic descent and the royal dignity of Jesus. Just as Saint Luke was to echo in the song of the angelic choir the promise of salvation to all mankind, so Saint Matthew reports the words of the angel to Joseph: "Thou shalt call his name Jesus, for he shall save his people from their sins" (I; 21). It is in the same spirit that Matthew chose the events of which we read in his account of the childhood of Christ—it was Jesus whom the angel announced to Joseph and whom the Magi came to worship—and he, who, pursued by Herod with such hatred, was the King of the Jews, the Messiah promised by God to Israel.

From the viewpoint of the historian, perhaps what lends greatest weight to the truthfulness of these chapters is the exactitude of detail in which they abound. For example, it is entirely true that the Magi, who were Persian priests, were particularly devoted to the study of the stars, and therefore the notion of a star announcing a major event is quite ap-

propriately introduced. Even more striking is the figure of
Herod. Saint Matthew paints him exactly as we know him
from other sources, extremely mistrustful of others and always
ready to suspect them of plotting to menace his throne. He
was, as well, extremely quick to rid himself of anyone he
feared. The murder of a few dozen children is not more
surprising by a man such as Herod than is his destruction of
his wife Mariamne, his brother-in-law, three of his own children, and many others; and all of these murders are facts
beyond contention. From the historical point of view, there
is no reason to doubt that the Persian astrologers undertook
a long journey in order to investigate the birth of a child
whose destiny gave promise of being an extraordinary one.
And there is even less reason to doubt that the despot at
Jerusalem would have ordered a massacre of all newborn
children. It is therefore quite natural that a biographical
study of Mary finds place for these events and their consequences.

FOUR

THE MOST RETIRING OF
CHARACTERS

THERE IS BUT A HANDFUL OF DOCUMENTS to mark the starting point for the loving curiosity of the Christian who goes in search of the Mother of God. How little material is here! And how natural seems the wish of the primitive Christian community, of the devout who desired to peer beneath the surface in order that they might more clearly limn the lines of her appealing image. But this effort at deeper penetration may tend toward error. Saint Louis Grignion de Montfort, who was greatly devoted to Our Lady, has said that the greater mysteries which encompass "this admirable being" ought to remain mysteries, precisely because the world is incapable of piercing them, is unworthy of penetrating them. Although our contemplation of Mary must remain clouded by "uncertainty and by many unanswered questions" yet even this may serve to keep it, as Père Régamey has profoundly remarked, "just sufficiently darkened so that the eyes of the heart, illumined by faith and love, may strive all the better to fulfill their task." It is, of course, the privilege of the arts to surround the image of Mary with all their magical insights and infinitely varied suggestiveness. This, according to Saint Thomas, is also a mode of knowing. But in the more practical workaday sphere, moderation and reserve are necessities: we have no right to press for too great exactitude in a matter which the Holy Spirit has willed to be rather allusive and sketchy than completely revealed.

The personal reserve characteristic of Mary is quite of a piece with the reserve shown by the texts of Scripture which tell us of her. Let us take into consideration, for example, the most remarkable of all the psychological concepts which are expressed through her, that of a Virgin who is a Mother, a young girl who conceived in a fashion so exceptional that it defies analysis. The texts of Holy Writ do not linger upon this for more than a moment. Unlike the authors of the Apocrypha who, as we shall see, feel it necessary to comment upon the fact, even to attempt to demonstrate its truth by markedly singular means, the four inspired writers treat delicately what they well know to be a mystery. How great is the restraint shown by Saint Luke in his account of the Annunciation and the virginal conception which followed it! How modestly expressed, as Saint Matthew sets it down, is the statement of the doubt which troubled Saint Joseph! Never do we find anything to indicate that during the public life of Christ the hidden secret of his birth was flaunted abroad; on the contrary, with what artlessness do the Evangelists state that Joseph was commonly thought to be his father! The unfathomable mystery of fecund virginity can be perceived only in light given by God, and it was in that light that the Evangelists were content to let it remain.

Therefore, it is quite impossible to analyze the psychology

[29]

of Mary in the way that a novelist or a biographer attempts to treat that of any other woman. How many are the commentators who have tried to re-create what this mother thought when, knowing what she knew, she saw her little boy at play, or later when, lost in the crowd, she saw him as a man who was carrying out his mission to preach the Word. How many have endeavored to depict that combination of joys and terrors which reached its climax when the devastating sorrow of standing by the cross of her Son mingled with a hope which was unquenchable in the innermost heart of this elect being. Faith and poetry alike have sought and found wondrous tones to embroider these themes; but these are no more than merely human interpretations, and each of us, indeed, has the privilege of attempting them in the silence of his own heart.

It seems that the texts tell us nothing about events in the life of this Mother which do not appear to be closely connected with the mystery of her essential vocation. For example, there is no document from which we may learn her feeling for Saint Joseph, for that spouse who had shown himself so generous and so trusting. If we are permitted to picture her as a tender and loving wife, there is, nonetheless, not a line in the Gospel to furnish us with any information on this most human element in her character. Even Christian art has obeyed, with wonderful respect, the reticence due her, and has never sought to raise the veil from this aspect of her life, voluntarily leaving out of account certain means of depicting Mary the woman and her womanly traits.

So it is that psychologically one knows the Virgin Mary only by those virtues which are hers. And she practices these virtues in a manner marked by supernatural modesty and by a reserve which surrounds them with a halo of grace that makes them even more beautiful than they would otherwise be. It is indeed in their fullness, in their absolute perfection, that she manifests them—she is the complete incarnation of virtue.

What the words of Saint Luke and the simple phrases of her conversation with the angel reveal is a clarity of soul unshadowed by the slightest taint of evil, a depth of character which is inwardly convinced of its high destiny, and a physical integrity which is unquestionable and cannot be challenged. Does not this afford us a vision of the very pattern of virginity, a virginity before which all other virginity, no matter how noble, is lessened? It is in Mary that humanity has always lovingly recognized that the ideal of the pure young maiden achieved perfect expression. She is that young maiden of the annunciation whom, for more than fifteen centuries, Western devotion has pictured as possessing the fullness of that unsated urge to be pure which burns within our hearts, which was the star of our childhood, and which life, little by little, betrays. The graceful air of one of Giotto's Virgins arouses in our souls a sense of a region never encroached upon, a state untouched by fault or flaw, a secret spot that we feel for an instant to be within ourselves—where absolute honesty resolves all the contradictions of our nature, and where to be pure means to be wise and loving.

The reply framed by the lips of this young maiden to the angel's astonishing greeting is indeed no more than the perfect expression of the virtue—whose other name is hope—which arouses in us submission to the Divine Will: "May it be done unto me according to thy Word!" This is the equivalent of the *fiat voluntas tua* (Thy Will be done) murmured by Jesus in the depths of his human misery, or of those striking words which old Simeon sang in prophetic joy:

"Into thy hands, O Lord, I commend my spirit." As Msgr. Romano Guardini has put it, an extraordinary suggestion had been made to Mary; [1] she was required, as it were, to catapult herself into the dark unknown by putting herself in God's hands. She did this with a largeness of soul which shows her selflessness. There is no evidence that she held back, that she feared to make this "leap"; for no sooner had she understood the import of the angel's message, than her heart overflowed with acceptance of it. Not for an instant did she think to hide herself from it, and in her the virtue of hope attained heights of all but inaccessible perfection; her whole being was established in acceptance of God's will.

Once the miraculous happening had taken place and the Child had been born, it is the virtues of motherhood which rise up and flourish in Mary. Theologians, poets, and commentators of every kind have subjected to analysis the maternal feelings of her who had given birth to the God-Man; they have been ready to imagine that she herself did not grasp this mystery, that she remained sunk in stupor before it. The actuality which shows itself in the text of the Gospel is very much more simple and more moving; for, from the moment she became a mother, Mary was completely absorbed in her maternity. As we see her covering her newborn child with swaddling clothes, see her carrying him in her arms on the journey into Egypt, and twelve years later, as we follow her in her distress while she searches for the little boy she believes lost, we see the mother exercising motherly virtues and prerogatives, fulfilling that inherent obligation of motherhood which dictates that her life and the life of her child be one. Here is the highest ideal of womanhood, when she

[1] R. Guardini: *Le Seigneur,* I; 17, in the French translation. [English translation by Elinor Castendyke Briess, *The Lord* (Chicago: © Regnery, 1954).]

understands how to grasp it and how freely to embrace it. This is what Peter Wust definitively expressed when he wrote of "The Ideal of Service": "Woman's chief privilege does not rest in the *de facto* act of serving itself: it consists rather in the holy right she possesses in her readiness to serve; and it is thus that she restores to *service* its highest sense. This is a privilege which is shared by womankind with divinity; for in the Godhead is maternity in the absolute sense. It is Love's thirst for the Absolute. The great privilege of woman that cannot be taken from her is the capacity to serve; and in its highest form this capacity is called Motherhood." [2]

Therefore, those few episodes in the public life of Our Lord in which allusion is made to Mary—all of which serve to show a separation between them—must be judged from the point of view of maternal virtue in its highest form. True motherhood is not only a full acceptance of sorrow and suffering, it implies a permanent and deliberate effacement of self. Not for themselves, nor for their own pleasure, do mothers bring their children to birth. As her Son seems as if he were going to thwart her at Cana, as she is declared to be no more than an abstraction to whom the Son of Man indicates he prefers his disciples and followers, is Mary not then the model of the everlasting Mother who knows well that the ties must be broken between herself and him who has grown from her flesh in order that the man she has brought into the world may fulfill his mission in life? The apocryphal writers have grasped neither the mystery nor the depth of Christ's attitude to Mary. Nor did they understand how some of his replies, seemingly of an unexpected sort, do not actually

---

[2] Peter Wust: *La mission métaphysique de la femme*, in *Problèmes de la sexualite*. "Présences," Paris: Plon 1937. [cf. also Auguste Valensin, S.J.: *Joy in the Faith;* translated by Alastair Guinan. (New York: © Desclée Company, 1959), pp. 38-39.]

sunder Mother and Son; for in reality they weld them together in submission to a destiny bigger than either of them, a destiny which expresses the Divine Will. Although he summoned the Twelve to the Last Supper, to the Sacramental Eucharist—and the Twelve included Judas—Our Lord did not summon his Mother! Can we not discern here the very apex of motherly effacement?

And when, at length, all was about to be accomplished, when Jesus was hanging on the Cross, the extraordinary restraint of the Gospel text evidently corresponds to a psychological attitude intended to serve as a pattern. During the course of the centuries, artists have often painted that moment of dreadful dereliction, that moment of an agony which had moved along, step by step, with Christ's own agony, as the Virgin half faints in sorrow. Yet despite the beauty of the masterpieces which draw their inspiration from this theme they are but interpretations and imaginings. Had Mary fainted on Calvary, John would certainly have said so. Instead, he forthrightly declares: "Mary stood by the Cross." All Mary's strength of soul, all her hope is summed up in these few words; and Claudel perceived this when in his *L'Épée et le Miroir* he compared the figure of the Sorrowful Mother to the "valiant woman" of the Scripture. "Not only did she stand in the physical sense; it was her soul, as well, which held itself upright!" A real mother, who sees her child in the grip of the final catastrophe, has other things to do than abandon herself to grief. She is watchful of herself and she strives to keep up her courage lest she add to her child's distress the sight of her own. The way in which she may now serve her Son is to be quiet, to hold herself in hand, to restrain her tears, serving him by self-sacrifice. This idea of Mary's demeanor is certainly more worthy of her than that presented by those painters of suffering, Duccio, Van der Weyden, and Grünewald, beautiful as their works are.

The chief psychological characteristics of Our Lady are purity, submissiveness to God's will, the spirit of sacrifice and of willingness to forget herself in self-effacement, and strength of soul in sorrow. It is along these lines that we define the ideal woman in a sense which cannot be surpassed. If we are to adhere to the text of the Gospel, no further commentary is possible; but just as it is, it is enough to arouse our reverence.

FIVE

A LOWLY JEWISH MAIDEN

CAN WE, WITHOUT OVERWORKING or unduly enlarging it, add a few details to this portrait? Is this to be done by thinking not of individualistic characteristics but of things determined according to general circumstances of time, place, and surroundings during Mary's lifetime? Historically, the period of Our Lady's childhood, when the miraculous event foretold by the Annunciation took place and she brought her son into the world, is one of the best-known in the ancient world. The Jewish historian, Flavius Josephus, has set down for us minute details of the era, and we can establish with precision what were the customs and manners of those who lived in Israel. On the one hand, we have a source of information in the Old Testament, for we know that its legalistic prescriptions were most strictly adhered to by these most formalistic of peoples. On the other hand, we may properly refer also to the information furnished by the Talmud, for although that great Jewish document was not actually written until a later time, we may legitimately argue that the characteristic Jewish legalism and formality would insure that the customs which are so minutely set forth in the Mishna are such as had endured unchanged for two or three centuries before they were written down. Therefore, although we cannot possibly know all the concrete details about Mary as an individual, we may, nevertheless, very easily picture the life of a simple Jewish maiden of her era, and we may thus come to an awareness of the kind of figure she is likely to have cut among her contemporaries.

The very first thing that suggests itself to us as we read the Gospel and seek help from the Old Testament in interpreting it, is the remarkable knowledge which Our Lady appears to have had of the Sacred Scripture. In that wonderful poem, the *Magnificat*, which came to her lips in reply to her cousin Elizabeth's greeting, there is not a line which is not full of allusive references to the Bible. Whole passages are citations or paraphrases from the Scriptures, and recall, almost word for word, such passages as the canticle sung by Anna, the mother of Samuel, when she learned that the Lord had taken pity on her barrenness (Kings I; 2). Phrases like "my spirit hath exulted in God my Saviour . . ." and "He, . . . mindful of his mercy . . ." come directly from the Psalms (CXI; 9, CIII; 28, 29, etc. . . .) or from the Prophets where similar passages are to be found (for example, in Habacuc III; 18 or Joel II; 21, or Isaiah II; 17). It is impossible to conceive of a more all-pervading influence, of a more total impregnation by scriptural sources.

Nonetheless, it would doubtless be going too far to see here an exceptional tendency, restricted to Mary alone. It is to be admitted, of course, that this knowledge of the sacred text would be something of "second nature" to one so privileged as was Mary, a being devoted to God from the beginning of her existence. Yet we must recall that the whole of life

among Jews of every station was wound up with the Scriptures, and that reference to its text was a commonplace of
life, as is indeed true of the verses of the Koran among the
Moslems. Children at the school of the synagogue, the *beth-
hasepher,* did the bulk of their studies under the direction of
the *hassan,* or cantor, by repeating Biblical texts; and in the
streets and squares of the towns, it was a common sight to see
a Doctor of the Law explaining some passage of the Holy
Book to a group of attentive listeners. Mary's familiar use of
the sacred texts is, like Our Lord's own use of them, something common to her people and her time rather than being
peculiarly characteristic of her as an individual.

She was a young Jewish maiden who, externally, seemed
like many another. The very name that she bore, Miriam,
which has become Mary through its Latin form, was then of
all names the most common in Palestine. Of six or seven
women spoken of in the Gospel, five are so called: the Mother
of Jesus, Mary Clophas, Mary Salome, Mary Magdalene, and
Mary, the mother of Mark. It no longer meant "the beloved
of the Lord" as it had in the time of Moses when his sister
was so named (under the form "Mirya"). It was now taken,
more modestly, to signify something like "good woman";
it was a name much used by ordinary people, and princesses
were no longer called by it.

Yet, despite this, was Mary not a princess? Was she not a
descendant of David, an offspring of the royal line? The
Angel recalled this to her when he declared of the Child that
would be born to her that God would give to him the throne
of David, his father. Even had Saint Matthew (I; 1-17) and
Saint Luke (III; 23-38) not affirmed it, this Davidic descent
of the Virgin Mary is certainly part of the tradition of the
Primitive Church. Saint Paul appears to refer to it (Rom. I;

[38]

3); [1] and the Fathers of the Church, whenever they speak of Mary do so as well. It was this notion which inspired the artists of the Middle Ages when they depicted the Tree of Jesse. But as a matter of fact, the historical explanation is less imposing than these artistic representations. It was a natural consequence of the large harems of David and Solomon that the royal descendants were numerous. Not all were charged with responsibility, riches, and dignity. In the days of the Maccabees, the existence of numerous heirs of the Davidic family served to restrain the glorious brothers from readily assuming the crown; and when, much later, Domitian the emperor (81-96), heard of the prophecy which promised a throne to the children of King David and caused the last representatives of the royal line of Israel to be brought before him, he found the poor country people who were led in (in the persons of the two grandsons of Jude the Apostle), to be so lowly and so inoffensive that he granted them their lives and sent them back to their farming. Therefore, it would be at variance with the truth to represent the child of David as being necessarily of princely bearing, and the picture which the Gospel gives us of a daughter of the people is, from the historian's viewpoint, the more likely one.

There is then every probability that the usages and customs of the humbler classes of the Jews were those of Mary. We shall best picture her in the framework of the latter days of the Jewish community. When she was born, and during her childhood, Palestine was ruled by Herod the Great. At the time of her birth, it was but twenty years since the Edomite had been given the whole of the Promised Land by Octavius

[1] On the question of the genealogies of Joseph and Mary, consult the second chapter of *Jesus and His Times* by Henri Daniel-Rops; English translation by Ruby Millar (New York: © E. P. Dutton & Co., Inc., 1954), pp. 114-116.

[39]

and Antony who were then acting in concert, but he had never been fully accepted by all religious Jews. The child Mary would certainly have heard various things about the despotic prince, things carried about by those "little birds" which spread rumors of his crimes, of his amorous adventures, of his political cunning, and of his luxurious habits. Later she would certainly have heard of that great enterprise proclaimed by Herod in the very year of her birth, when he announced his intention to rebuild the Temple. As Mary grew up the Temple was rising; and the parallelism here has its own symbolic value for the meditative heart. For the faithful Jews in whose eyes the Temple was something of fundamental importance, the fact of its reconstruction became a subject of continual discussion. As far away as the outlying villages they would speak of the immense labor of widening the square before the Temple, of the ten thousand workmen put to the task, the rare stones and precious woods, and the quantities of gold which were carried constantly into the workyard. Mary must have been about twelve years old when the solemn opening, the Dedication, took place at Pentecost in the year 10 B.C., in the midst of a crowd of spectators and to the accompaniment of an unheard of degree of magnificence. It is not impossible that she may have been present, either because she accompanied her parents as was customary, or because, according to the tradition preserved in the Apocrypha, she actually lived in the Temple.

Up to the time of the birth of Jesus, the life of the Virgin was probably shadowed from afar by that of the despot; for Jesus, as we know, was born about six years before our era, and Herod the Great died in 4 B.C. At the time of her betrothal, Mary may have heard much of the great events which marked the end of the reign, of the tragic misunderstanding between the old King and his son, Antipater. A great deal of talk must have circulated in all the little villages of Palestine regarding the decrepit old tyrant, growing more violent and cruel as he hastened on to his death, his hair and beard dyed and his body wasted by some mysterious ailment.

Mary was about fourteen or fifteen years at the oldest when she was betrothed to Joseph. It was at this age that the daughters of Israel married. As soon as they were marriageable they became engaged, and it was common for a woman of thirty to be a grandmother. According to the Talmud "man was created that he might procreate." Both Old and New Testaments demonstrate the primary importance attached to fruitfulness, and the opprobrium in which barren women were held. Obviously, this obligation to marry, which the law and custom of the Jewish people laid upon all women, was one which raised a serious question in Mary's case.

The reply which she made to the Angel: "How shall this be, seeing that I know not man?" would be meaningless unless it meant that she had made up her mind never to know man, that in other words, as Catholic faith expresses it, she had made a vow of virginity. Vows were regarded as having an important place in the lives of a people who were as strict as the Jews in the practice of their religion. In Deuteronomy (XXIII, 22, 24), Ecclesiastes (V, 3, 5), as well as in certain other parts of the Holy Scripture, attention is given to vows and to the matter of their regulation. In particular, it is known that Nazarites bound themselves, for a specified time, to observe chastity and certain forms of abstinence, and to restrain from cutting their hair. But did there exist a vow for women similar to that of the Nazarites among the men? Could it be possible, moreover, that such a vow would be accorded any real value inasmuch as it ran counter to the normal precept: "Increase and multiply." In the Mishna there is to be read a Talmudic text which formally declares: "No one may vow to transgress the precepts of the Law." This aspect of Jewish custom makes us realize how extraordinary and exceptional was Mary's vow of virginity.[2]

Apart from this, the information which can be gathered about marriages among the Jews confirms what the Gospel tells us. Considering his wisdom and prudence, it seems likely that Joseph was already a man of mature years; and this seems confirmed by the fact that he died before the public life of Our Lord began. It is certain that such marriages between persons of widely differing ages were in vogue among the Jews. For legal reasons (the Talmud cites certain cases) an uncle could marry his niece, or even his grandniece. Therefore the marriage of a grown man to a child of thirteen or fourteen—as is common nowadays among the Arabs—would amount to no more than a solemn engagement. "Mary was espoused to Joseph"—these words indicate that there had been established between them a contractual state wholly unlike what we mean by an "engagement." According to our law—civil and religious alike—marriage constitutes the only binding act and contract; and breach of promise but rarely gives right to a claim for reparation, unless there be a question of scandal and prejudice. On the contrary, the Hebrews gave espousals a force very close to that of marriage, and espousals conferred all the rights of marriage with the exception of the right of access to the body. In the case of virgins it was for one year, in the case of widows it was for one month, that the betrothed woman was regarded as being under the jurisdiction of the man to whom she was promised. Even though, in

---

[2] So it is that some of the apocryphal writers, having grasped the problem perfectly, thought that the case of Mary was referred to the Doctors of the Law or to the Assembly of the People.

such cases, conjugal relations were, in principle, forbidden them, the Talmud informs us that they were frequently entered into; and the husband might actually come to knowledge of his wife at the home of his father-in-law. A child born under such circumstances was regarded as being legitimate. During this pre-nuptial time, there was a strict obligation that the parties to the contract be faithful to each other. Infidelity was considered as equivalent to adultery, and if an espoused maiden were denounced as an adulteress by her husband, she could not escape the punishment of death. According to the prescriptions of Deuteronomy (XXII; 23-24) it was stated in formal terms: "If a man have espoused a damsel that is a virgin, and someone find her in the city and lie with her, Thou shalt bring them both out to the gate of that City, and they shall be stoned . . ." In the light of these Jewish customs, it may be concluded that the mere signs of pregnancy in Mary during the period of her betrothal were not of themselves sufficient, in the eyes of the people, to destroy her reputation: it would be necessary that Joseph accuse her before she could be convicted of guilt, a guilt subjecting her to death. These considerations emphasize the significance of the inward crisis which took place within the heart of this just man, a crisis which the Gospel, despite the restraint of its language, brings vividly before us.

Beyond this, the details which may be gleaned from Jewish sources are of slight account, and they add only to our knowledge of external affairs. It is a simple matter to form an idea of the houses in which Mary lived as a child and as a young wife. These houses were half cavelike structures similar to those seen in Palestine today, fixed upon a hillside and having their foundations in the chalk of a grotto. In this grotto or cave would ordinarily be found the kitchen, with its furnace, spit and grill and large vessels for the storing of provisions, as well as bottles and baskets. There may also be pictured the chests in which were kept veils, mantles, tunics, and girdles, as well as the more numerous articles of apparel of the man of the family. Mary's clothing is something of which we know a good deal. It would be of wool in winter and of linen in summer, and it would consist of two garments worn one over the other like a chemise and a robe or gown; a veil would cover her head in the traditional fashion, for it was looked upon as unbefitting to be seen without the veil in the streets; her feet would generally be bare or covered with simple sandals of wood or of leather. On festivals she would wear richer clothing, more flowing in line, and on her head would be a kind of filet adorned with a picture of Jerusalem. This was called "the ornament of the golden city."

Mary's food and that which she would prepare for her spouse and her child was that of the Palestinians of her day, and would consist of barley (rather than wheat) made into bread or biscuits, lentils prepared with oil or honey, onions (great quantities of onions), beans, asparagus, tomatoes, large radishes marinated in wine, and sometimes there would be plates of rice which had come in the caravans. There would be a great deal of fruit—peaches, plums, pears, figs, melons, dates and pomegranates—but very little meat; some fish in better times, and certain fritters heavy with honey and oil and fried in the same fashion as they are prepared today when eaten in Eastern lands.

It was a simple life, full each day of the same tasks endlessly repeated, and scarcely differing from the life of a peasant in Western society. There would be water to draw, bread to knead and bake in the oven, meals to prepare, and clothes to mend. Her work-basket at her side, Mary would

[44]

sit mending all afternoon, if she were not spinning. From time to time, the Child playing near her would call: "Mommie! Mommie!" There would be but one constant interruption of her appointed tasks: at least three times a day she would resort to prayer by saying the prescribed psalms and blessings. On the Sabbath all work was set aside, and men and things alike were as if prostrate before Almighty God. Life was a round of monotonous tasks patiently undertaken, and the only interruption in the course of duty came with the great festivals of which there were many in the Jewish calendar. On these days the people would either gather together in the local congregation, or even go up to Jerusalem, there to take part in the traditional liturgical ceremonies. Apart from these feasts and from weddings and other family celebrations, there were not many distractions.

Such was Mary's life, and it went on in this fashion for thirty years. The death of Joseph would not have caused any change in her manner of living apart from her donning the dark weeds of widowhood. Henceforth, it was her son who was the head of the house, and responsible for providing for their support. All of these details unite to form for us a fondly familiar setting in which we can picture the Holy Virgin: how like our own mothers and wives now seems the woman chosen by God to bring to pass the greatest of His works! How clearly does her humanity appear!

SIX

QUESTIONS WITHOUT ANSWERS

Nevertheless, if we are to restrict ourselves to the documents we have named, it must be admitted that certain questions do arise in our minds for which no ready answers are forthcoming. The most cursory reader of the Holy Scriptures will readily agree that there is no mention whatever in the Gospel of a great many details which a thousand recollections of his childhood have imprinted on his memory. As we look at our Christmas cribs, so charming and so poetically appealing, we may wonder why the place in which the figures of the Provençal *santons* [1] are set is represented to be a grotto, while Saint Luke speaks quite bluntly of a stable? Why are the ox and the ass inevitably associated with the picture? That these lowly beasts are there as representatives of God's creation is a touching piece of symbolism; but what basis has this in the Gospel text? And why, above all, has custom decreed that the Magi are to be called "kings"? Why this pretentious precision

[1] Interesting details and pictures of these little figures of people from the countryside, costumed in a manner descriptive of their occupations, appear in Maurice Vloberg: *Les Noëls de France* (Grenoble: Arthaud, 1938); pp. 190-193.

[46]

unknown to Saint Matthew? Why, again, why the *names* of Gaspar, Melchior, and Balthasar, names of which the Gospel says nothing?

In respect to Mary questions arise which are even more pointed. These are suggested not merely by popular traditions; they stem, rather, from the Church's liturgy. So it is that on August 16, we celebrate the feast of "Saint Joachim, Father of the Blessed Virgin Mary" and on July 26, that of "Saint Anne," her Mother. Now the only information furnished by the Gospel about Mary's parents is found in the verse in which Saint John tells us that at the foot of the Cross there stood by Mary's side "Mary of Clophas, the sister of his Mother." Of course, this may be interpreted as saying that Clophas was the husband of a sister of Our Lady, or as suggesting that one of the parents of Our Lady had been twice married, in which case Mary of Clophas would be her half-sister.

What is even more astonishing is the thought that some of the great festivals of Our Lady are of very uncertain origin. An example is that of November 21, the Presentation of Our Lady in the Temple. This has long been a favorite in the Christian East. The Byzantine emperor, Michael Commeneus, mentions it in an official document of 1166, and Philippe de Mazières, a Frenchman attached to the Court of the King of Cyprus, when sent by his royal master to Avignon in 1372, was so enthusiastic in his description of this feast that Gregory XI introduced it into the Roman liturgy. Even better known, nowadays, is the festival which ranks among some Catholics as the highest of all Our Lady's feasts, the solemnity held on August 15, when every country church in France is filled with spectators of that Procession commemorating the vow made in 1638 by Louis XIII, who desired that there should be recalled annually the fact that on that day he had placed his people and his kingdom under the tutelage of the Mother of Mercy. Now the Assumption of Our Lady is something unknown to the Gospel, nor is it mentioned at all in the book of the Acts of the Apostles which says nothing whatever of Mary after Pentecost.

It is not in our personal imaginations alone that these questions arise: works of art, in every age, raise their echoes and even suggest newer problems. Any attempt to present a "Life of Our Lady in Works of Art" would have to take into account a considerable number of scenes and situations for which there is no evident warrant in the words of the New Testament. How great is the knowledge which artists exhibit in respect to her parents! Not only do they know them to have been called Anne and Joachim, but they give the impression that they are aware as well that Mary's birth was miraculous, in the same way as was that of John the Baptist, born to the aged Elizabeth. A mosaic at Daphne in Greece portrays this miracle in majestic fashion, and the "Meeting at the Golden Door" was a theme destined to be treated frequently during the Middle Ages and up to the time of the Renaissance.[2] Artists show Mary to us in her childhood, as in the delightful incident of her Presentation in the Temple, beloved by Titian, by Van der Weyden, by Carpaccio.[3] Artists know, too, and they tell us, that Mary lived in

[2] [This encounter of Anne and Joachim is based upon a passage in *Pseudo-Matthew*. There is a representation of it in the Pinakotek at Munich by the Master of the Passion of Lyversberg, a painter of the fifteenth century German School. Joachim, having been told by an angel to leave his flocks and return to the city, meets his wife at the Golden Gate and embraces her tenderly on learning that she is to have a child.—A.G.]

[3] [Inspiration for this scene, where Mary is shown ascending the steps of the Temple while the High Priest awaits to receive her, is again from the Apocrypha which may, as M. Daniel-Rops suggests (p. 212 of the French edition), be themselves echoing the words of Ecclesiasticus, applied in the liturgy to Mary, ". . . in the holy dwelling place I have ministered before him" (Ecclus. 24; 14).—A.G.]

the Temple like a little nun, that she prayed and wove the
veil of the Sanctuary. So much is, indeed, pictured for us
by a fifth century tombstone found at Arles and now in the
crypt of the Madeleine at Saint Maximin-du-Var. This may
be the oldest representation of Our Lady in France. Mary is
pictured in the classical attitude of prayer and she wears a
veil which falls from her shoulders in full folds. The inscrip-
tion, in Low Latin, is: *Maria Virgo, Minester de Tempulo
Gerosale,* "Mary the Virgin, serving in the Temple at
Jerusalem." The notion underlying this work of art is evidently to be found in the sixth chapter of *Pseudo-Matthew.*
The same representation is repeated on a piece of embroidery
on a beautiful medieval cope. Why do we find these unexpected details on the margin of the authentic text of the
Gospel? Why is the Annunciation sometimes depicted by the
side of a fountain? And why, also, was the earlier annunciation supposed to have been made to Anne, depicted as well
by a fountain? What can be the origin of that bizarre fashion
in which the advent of the divine promise is given material
form in the shape of a naked child borne toward the Virgin
on a shaft of light which stems from the lips of the Father
in the magnificent and mysterious altar screen at Aix-en-
Provence? [4] And we may as well go on to ask what can be
the meaning of that sculpture in relief by Orcagna at Or San
Michele and of the Grecian mosaics of Raphael or Benozzo
Gozzoli, which show Saint Joseph at the time of his marriage
and depict the strange incident of a dove going forth from

[4] [The allusion is to the fifteenth century painting by the Master of the
Annunciation of Aix at the Church of the Madeleine at Aix-en-Provence. In
this most curious depiction of the scene, a ray of light having its origin in
the mouth of God the Father falls upon Mary who kneels below, and in
the midst of the ray is seen the body of a little child. This may be no more
than an attempt to depict the Incarnation in a concrete way or it may be,
as M. Daniel-Rops suggests, an example of an heretical interpretation of the
dogma, based upon some details found in the Apocrypha.—A.G.]

[49]

his staff? In the lovely Nativity scene which is in the Museum of Dijon, a painting by the fifteenth century Master of Mérode, two matrons are to be seen whom we should not expect to find in the picture. One of them is shown behaving in a manner which is even more surprising than is her presence.[5] Continuing, we should have to look into the origin of those evocations of Mary "falling asleep in the Lord" which were so dear to the hearts of the artists who depicted Our Lady. These Assumption scenes are repeated from age to age, ever being given new form by talent or genius. Whence came that coronation scene which inspired the brethren of Limbourg,[6] Fra Angelico, and Velásquez to the creation of what may be the masterpiece of each? And so we would come to that great picture of the Virgin as Mediatrix, where she is shown interceding for men before her Son enthroned in glory, a picture in which we have what may be the finest example of the delicate art of the French manuscript painters.[7]

[5] [This is evidently an attempt to depict what M. Daniel-Rops later describes as "the scabrous incident" of the midwife who wanted to test Mary's virginity and whose hand, according to the twentieth chapter of the *Protevangelium,* was destroyed by fire. There is an interesting allusion to this in the recent work of Dom Joseph Lemarié, *La Manifestation du Seigneur* (Paris: Les Éditions du Cerf, 1957); p. 256, n. 1, and plate opposite.—A.G.]

[6] In the Musée de Chantilly is preserved the manuscript called *Les Très Riches Heures du Duc de Berry* wherein the *Coronation of the Virgin* is depicted in a miniature of Pol de Limbourg and his brothers (fifteenth century), instinct with a poetry elsewhere perhaps unequalled.

[7] In a fifteenth century French manuscript of the *Légende dorée* (No. 244 in the Bibliothèque Nationale at Paris) Mary is shown in prayer before the Holy Trinity.

SEVEN

STRANGE ANSWERS FROM THE
APOCRYPHA

IF AN ATTEMPT SHOULD BE MADE to find an answer to these
questions in some documentary source—although, as we shall
see, such a compulsion is far from being universally felt—
there do actually exist some documents which furnish answers, and they are documents which come to us from Christian antiquity. The apocryphal writings offer abundant
examples of attempts to reply to these queries. The eleventh
chapter of the *Protevangelium Jacobi*,[1] tells us specifically
that it was at the fountain that the Angel appeared to Mary,
and in the eighteenth chapter we learn further that just as
the holy birth was about to occur "Joseph came upon a grotto
and brought Mary into it." This information is repeated by
Pseudo-Matthew. In the manuscripts of the *Gospel of the
Infancy* we discover that the mysterious Magi who knelt
before the newborn Child and his Virgin Mother are called
"kings" and are given specific names. If we seek a textual

---

[1] In the second part of the present work the reader will find the chief
apocryphal texts to which reference is made here.

[51]

source for the picture, presented to us by many artists, of the Presentation of the little Mary, a baby of three, in the Temple of the Lord, as she serenely walks across the Holy Court without a backward glance at her parents, we shall find it again in the *Protevangelium* (chapter VII) or in *Pseudo-Matthew,* where an account of these happenings is given. Similarly, in order to find a text narrating the earthly end of Our Lady and her Assumption into heavenly glory, we must have recourse to one or another of those apocryphal books which bear such titles as *The Book of the Passing of the Blessed Mary,* or to some similar work such as the famous *Transitus Mariae.*

Herein, indeed, are found explanations of most of the questions which certain works of art seem to raise. The meeting of Joachim and Anne at the Golden Gate is to be found in the third chapter of *Pseudo-Matthew;* and it is written, moreover, in beautiful style, with a degree of elevation which would not disfigure a chapter of Saint Luke. It is this document also which, in its seventh chapter, furnishes the details of the story of the staves held by those who aspired to Mary's hand; and we read that from the staff of Joseph "there went forth a dove, beauteous, and whiter than snow." The Master of Mérode was indebted to a most unpleasant and quite scabrous passage in the Apocrypha when he introduced the figures of the unlooked-for midwives into the painting which is now in the Museum at Dijon.

One might well imagine that the curious detail of the altar screen of Aix-en-Provence, where the small figure of a child is shown coming toward the Virgin on a ray of light streaming from the lips of God the Father, was due to the artist's imagination, were it not for some concepts expressed in the Apocrypha. There is, for instance, a verse in *The As-*

[52]

cension of Isaiah (XI; 87), in which Mary and Joseph are described as being alone in their home when they suddenly see the newborn Infant at their side, while a passage in the Infancy Gospel tells how "the Word of God entered into Mary through her ear" (cf. p. 167, infra). In the same apocryphal text an incident is narrated in which the Child Jesus amuses himself by gliding along a shaft of sunlight.[2] One might go on to multiply these connections between art and the Apocrypha.

What, indeed, are these strange documents, written as it were on the margin of Holy Scripture and often seeming to show unexpected connections with the Scriptures? What is the meaning of the name Apocrypha? According to etymology, the Greek word *apocryphos* signifies "hidden" or "secret." Was this name given to these books in order to testify to some mysterious quality thought to mark their doctrine and source? It is not an easy matter to determine. Some thinkers who have been enamored of the esoteric have tried to present the Apocrypha as channels of certain ancient, secret, and deep traditions. The English scholar, E. de Bunsen, links them to nothing less than beliefs held in the Terrestrial Paradise which, after being transmitted to Persia or Bactriana, were gathered together by the Jews during their days of exile "by the streams of Babylon," and afterwards passed on by them to Jesus and His apostles.[3]

---

[2] "Jesus went forth to play with other children, and he talked with them. He led them to the house tops through the windows and dormers to where the sun was shining. And he said: 'Who is able to clasp one of the sunbeams and slide down on it from here to the ground below without hurting himself?' And no one of them could do this. Then he said: 'Look at me!' And clutching in his arms the rays of the sun, made of tiny glimmers of light, he slid down to the ground uninjured."

[3] E. de Bunsen: *The Hidden Wisdom of Christ and the Key of Knowledge or History of the Apocrypha.* 2 vols. (London: Longmans, Green, & Co., 1865).

In truth, this interpretation does not actually correspond to what is known of these documents nor to what one may gather from reading the texts themselves. They are almost wholly of a popular character, being even of a coarse nature. They are not at all illustrative of the gnostic or transcendentally metaphysical style. It seems very likely that the title of Apocrypha was given them at the time when, having been rejected by the Church, or at any rate being regarded by her with strong reservations, they were relegated to a subordinate position, marginal to Holy Writ and outside the body of works acknowledged to be marked by the signs of divine inspiration.

Even though sectarian groups did—as we shall see—make use of the Apocrypha to spread their characteristic doctrines, yet the Church could not employ them, for she has always been on the side of open expression of the truth, and has never practiced any system like the *arcana* or secret doctrine of the Eastern mystery religions. The very word *apocrypha* has a bad connotation in Christian ears. And, as a matter of fact, it early acquired a pejorative significance. Nowadays, the term is generally used to describe any literary work which by title or content pretends to take a place by the side of Holy Writ, but which has failed of acceptance by the Church. This meaning is very close to the definition given by the historian Rufinus in the fourth century: "Apocryphal Scriptures are those which the Fathers would not accept for use in public reading."

The proof that this was the usual meaning, and from the earliest ages that most commonly accepted, is found in the fact that there are numbered among the Apocrypha texts which have nothing secret about them, and whose authors are often well known and are irreproachably orthodox in doctrine. Such are *The Epistle Ascribed to Barnabas, The First Epistle of Saint Clement the Pope to the Corinthians,* and that extraordinary piece of mystical speculation called *The Pastor of Hermas.* All of these are books which are today studied among the works of the "Apostolic Fathers," and they are considered the first fruits of Christian literature.

But if we put on one side writings of this type, which might more correctly be termed *ecclesiastical literature,* we find that the whole body of the Apocrypha comprises even further categories. One finds texts like the *Gospel According to the Hebrews,* which seems to have been used in the earliest days of the Church and then to have been abandoned; others are more or less heretical. In these certain factions of Christians intertwined their own personal views of doctrinal matters with the authentic data of tradition: such are the *Gospel of Saint Peter,* the *Gospel of the Ebionites,* the *Gospel of Thomas,* the *Gospel of Philip,* and others. Finally, there are those texts—and it is these which bear upon our present subject—wherein popular curiosity, the folkloric propensity for the invention of tales, and elements of authentic tradition are all blended together in an inextricable muddle: such are the *Protevangelium of James, Pseudo-Matthew,* and the *Gospels of the Infancy,* the *Gospel of Nicodemus,* the books on the *Passing of Mary,* and *The History of Joseph the Carpenter,* all of which belong to this last division. We might add here that parallel to these "gospels" are to be found Acts of the Apostles and Apocalypse, likewise apocryphal and also composed according to the same diverse purposes.

It is difficult to feel at ease amidst the changing currents which characterize these writings. Their common note is that their texts, being free of regulation by the Church authorities, reflect myriad fancies and all sorts of tendencies.

[55]

They copy one from another, they contradict each other, they strive to surpass each other. Sometimes there is no resemblance between the Greek, Syriac, Coptic, Armenian, or Latin versions of the same document. One copyist may have chosen to conflate the text, another will have thought to edify the reader by omission. The end result is a state of complete confusion; and the number set by some at twenty-seven, by others at forty-five, as the total of these pseudo-gospels, cannot be taken quite seriously; for very often, the differences between them are but very slight. Paradoxically, it is by no means certain that further examples may not come to light in the future.

The matter of dating these writings is a more interesting question. Voltaire and, in his wake, the divines of Tübingen [4] declared the Apocrypha to be older than the Gospels. As a matter of fact, the bulk of them are of later date. They make explicit references to the canonical books, and sometimes they copy from them. On the other hand, certain of the Apocrypha are very ancient and owe their origin to oral tradition passed about by word of mouth in Palestine among the first Christians. One such example is the *Protevangelium Jacobi*. This was certainly known in the sixth century throughout the entire East, and its "gossipy" quality was commonly recognized in the third century when we find Clement of Alexandria alluding to it.[5] This flood of religious romance continued to grow during the third, fourth and fifth centuries, and new elements were constantly being introduced. The books devoted to the *Passing of Mary* are among the later writings. By this time the Church had long since made public declaration of the canon of Scripture, and had separated the wheat from the chaff.

4 Cf. the appendix, H. Daniel-Rops: *Jesus and His Times*.
5 For example, he alludes to the incident of the midwives in his *Stromata*.

Despite the illustrious names under which they sheltered themselves, these romantic texts were not received in the Church, which recognized as inspired no more than a definite number of writings whose apostolicity and catholicity were evident. Other texts were passed over and regarded with suspicion. Such were the Apocrypha. When Ludovico Antonio Muratori, Librarian of the Ambrosian at Milano, discovered and published, in 1740, a seventh century manuscript which recorded a list of scriptural books as recognized by the Church of Rome between the years 155 and 200, it was made clear that the Canon of Scripture, even in that ancient day, was more or less identical with our own Canon which is that promulgated by the Council of Trent. Nevertheless, this declaration of canonical status, thus early, did not prevent other writings of an apocryphal character from circulating in some form or other. Often enough they furnished material to the liturgical drama and were always favorites with story-tellers among the people. More and more, however, did the official Church become suspicious of them—Popes and Church Fathers exerted themselves firmly to keep such writings distinct from Holy Scripture. Saint Justin and Saint Irenæus both speak of the difference between the two kinds of writing; Tertullian is insistent on the question. Origen tells us that the Apocrypha have never been used in the public services of the Church; and Saint Athanasius, Saint Cyril of Jerusalem, Eusebius, and Saint John Chrysostom are of like mind. There is no doubt that as early as the fourth century and again during the pontificate of Innocent I at the beginning of the fifth century, there had been drawn up a catalogue of writings of a suspect character. A little later, during the sixth century, it was said that in the pontificate of Saint Gelasius (492-496) there had been issued a celebrated *Decree* concerning the use of Holy Scripture in the Church. This decree

[57]

contains what amounts to a list of "condemned" titles. So were the Apocrypha rejected.[6]

We therefore see that the Apocrypha are books which grew up, as it were, apart from the ordered currents of Christianity, and that the Church's attitude toward them has always been that they are best regarded as a body of literature which may not be entirely bad but which is to be received only with caution. This does not indicate that their place has been an insignificant one. Their importance is shown by the fact that such great Christian thinkers as Saint Irenæus, Tertullian, and Saint John Chrysostom have made them the subject of criticism. And, in any case, not every one of the Fathers of the Church always condemned them. In his *Stromata* we find Clement of Alexandria referring to the Apocrypha; and the great second century Roman teacher, Saint Justin, speaks of the *grotto* of the Nativity as of a fact generally admitted. In the third century, Origen, in his commentary on Matthew, mentions the opinion of those who explain the *brethren of Jesus* as his half-brothers, the children of the first marriage of Saint Joseph, and he cites the *Gospel of Peter* and the *Book of James* (which we call the *Protevangelium Jacobi*). Saint Gregory of Nyssa, one of the chief lights of the Cappadocian school of divines, is familiar with the Presentation of Mary in the Temple and with the grotto as the scene of the birth of Jesus. Many another example could be cited.

It is certain that even if the Apocrypha were not regarded as being what they professed to be, they continued to enjoy some circulation. "Try all things and keep whatever is found

---

[6] The fifth part of the Decree is *Notitia librorum apocryphorum qui nullatenus a nobis recipi debent,* i.e., a list of non-approved or unauthentic writings which in no wise ought be accepted among Christians as of scriptural authority. The word *Apocrypha* is here employed in the general sense as describing a book which has not been approved by the Church.

to be good"—this is the advice of Origen in such matters. The apocryphal documents were frequently hawked under the prestige of the name of Saint Jerome—a strange tribute to that testy scholar who was himself wary of fables but was to have the paternity of so many foisted upon him. Some elements in the Apocrypha which were not contrary to faith or morals were cherished by the Greek Church and Western travelers brought them back from the Orient with them.[7] Now disputed, again accepted, the data which the Apocrypha supplied served to replenish the popular storehouse of legendary lore and men continued to draw upon it. In the eleventh century it was only with evident regret that Fulbert of Chartres refused to accept these writings. In the thirteenth, Vincent of Beauvais, when writing his *Speculum majus,* would not grant authority to them, but he said that it is not forbidden to read them nor to believe things in them which are not contrary to the truths of faith. And down to the sixteenth century and the time of the Tridentine Council, this was the general feeling in the Church.

By referring to the *Speculum majus,* there is broached the main interest which these writings hold for us—their influence upon letters and the arts. Throughout the Middle Ages that influence is seen to be at work in countless ways, whether we turn to collections of sermons or to lives of the saints like those which were gathered together by Jacobus de Voragine in his *Legenda Aurea.*[8] Here are to be found whole sections of the Apocrypha, for example, large extracts from the *Liber*

---

[7] There are indications, even in Tibet, that the heretical Manicheans brought some apocryphal lore there with them.

[8] [The influence of this work upon English literature was assured by the appearance of the Caxton translation. In our own day a new translation has been published; see Jacobus de Voragine: *The Golden Legend;* translated and adapted by William Granger Ryan and Helmut Ripperger; 2 vols. (New York: © Longmans, Green, & Co., 1940).—A.G.]

Transitus Mariae. In the fifteenth century the *Vita Christi* embodied all that was recounted in the Apocrypha. Mystery and Miracle plays turned to them, and great poetry found them a source. Dante, for example, owes much to them in depicting his visions of the future life.

Through the medium of such literary works, Western medieval art came to know all these ideas and to react to their inspiration. As Abbé Migne remarks: "Were we to ignore the study of the apocryphal gospels, we would be unable to uncover the sources of Christian art. In them we find the well into which the artists dipped, after the death of the pagan legends, for that wealth of symbolic imagery developed during the Middle Ages." The wood-carvers and sculptors of our cathedrals were familiar with the *Speculum* or *Mirror* of Vincent of Beauvais; they knew, too, the *Golden Legend* of Jacobus de Voragine. M. Émile Mâle, in his great work *L'Art Réligieux en France,* has shown how great is the influence upon medieval imagery of apocryphal ideas as transmitted by these well-known books. Both the Christian primitives and the Renaissance painters who succeeded them were very well acquainted with the *Vita Christi,* and the influence of the pseudo-gospels is to be discerned in Van der Weyden or the Master of Mérode as well as in Raphael or Crivelli.

The Apocrypha fell into disfavor at the time of the Council of Trent and they have lost ground since the seventeenth century. Although Milton and Klopstock are notable among great writers for having continued to draw from these sources, the plastic arts seem to have turned completely away from them. The only episodes from the Apocrypha which maintained themselves in popular esteem were those which had been enshrined in the liturgy, although it is by no means certain, as we shall see, that they should have been put

there. Does this indicate a lessening of that yearning for
knowledge of the least detail of Holy Writ which was so
marked a feature of Christian thought in times when faith,
if stronger, was perhaps more naïve than our own? In any
event it seems that this aspect of Christian literature is
definitely behind us.

EIGHT

OUR LADY IN THE APOCRYPHA

THE PLACE OF OUR LADY in the whole body of the Apocrypha is a considerable one. Nor is this surprising, for the mystery of the Incarnation and that of Christ's divinity are closely linked to the special character of his Mother and to her unique virginity. The meagerness of detail which the canonical writings offer us supplied a reason to those who wished to remedy what they felt to be a deficiency: they misunderstood the admirable discretion of the canonical writers, and they added to, enlarged upon, and further embellished the little information we actually possess about the most self-effacing character in the New Testament.

Among the works of the apocryphal writers having to do with Mary, there are some which are particularly concerned with her and which appear to have been written in order to furnish more information about her life. Others tell of her only incidentally, as when they associate her with Our Lord or with Saint Joseph. Both are alike, however, in that they offer a transformed portrait of the retiring heroine whom we know from the narratives of Luke and Matthew.

The oldest of all the Apocrypha dealing with Mary is the *Protevangelium Jacobi.* The title signifies that this book aspires to offer a text antecedent to the Gospel, to be a sort of preface to Saint Luke, and it was as such that it was offered to the world in 1552 by the distinguished Orientalist, Guillaume Postel, who had discovered it in manuscript at Constantinople, and had made a Latin translation of it. Previously, in the Greek version, it had borne various titles of a more modest nature, such as, for example, *The Account of Mary's Birth,* written by James. The publication of the text in the sixteenth century and the quasi-official character which some pretended to accord to it, aroused other scholars to spirited disagreement. The learned Henri Estienne went so far as to declare that "by causing the publication of this book, the devil is making a laughing-stock of Christianity." Nevertheless, because of its literary form, marked by some degree of beauty, the direct and serious manner in which the tale is set forth and the deeply devotional spirit it expresses, this work seems certainly outstanding among all the apocryphal writings. If we overlook a detail here and there, this work may be described as being of all the Apocrypha closest to the high level of the canonical writings. The opening portion, which comprises the first sixteen chapters, recounts the miraculous birth of Mary after its announcement by an angel to her aged parents, Joachim and Anne, the Presentation of Mary in the Temple, and her Espousal to Joseph. Chapters XVII to XXI follow Saint Luke and Saint Matthew closely in the accounts of the birth of Jesus and of his adoration by the Magi. The end of this work (chapters XXII-XXIV) is concerned with the Massacre of the Innocents and the death of Zachary. These three sections are not all of the same date and it appears that the first portion, which is the

[63]

most interesting where Mary is concerned, may date from
130 or 140, which is about thirty years after the Fourth
Gospel was drawn up. In regard to the authorship of the
Protevangelium Jacobi no one now thinks that it might have
been written by James the Lesser, "the brother of the Lord"
who was the first bishop of Jerusalem. Whoever wrote it displays great lack of knowledge of the details of Jewish life and
he must have been an Oriental Greek. It was throughout the
East that this work was so well received and until the time of
Guillaume Postel it was known in the West only in a recast
form.[1]

The most noted of all these recastings is called the *Gospel
of Pseudo-Matthew*. Objection may be raised to this title, for
although some manuscripts attribute the work to Matthew,
others ascribe it to James or to John, and some even to
Onesimus, the slave on whose behalf Saint Paul wrote his
charming Epistle to Philemon. Generally, the work has been
presented as being a Latin translation, supposedly made by
Saint Jerome, from a document of apostolic times. As a
matter of fact, it is a work of the fifth, or even of the sixth
century put forth at a time when the name of Saint Jerome
was already so highly regarded that it lent respectability to
all sorts of outlandish extravagances. In the first portion the
author makes use of the *Protevangelium Jacobi* or of a similar
document, and he sets forth almost the same incidents, sometimes in greater detail.[2] Later, attention is given to the

---

[1] The oldest existing manuscript, in fragments, dates from the ninth
century and is in the Bibliothèque Nationale at Paris. This library also
possesses two manuscripts of the eleventh century. About fifty versions of the
Protevangelium in manuscript form are catalogued in various libraries.

[2] An example is seen in the story of Saint Joseph's staff which is much
more detailed than in the form in which it appears in the *Protevangelium*.
One manuscript differs very much from another, especially in the later recastings of the story. In the older versions a dove springs forth from the
staff, while in the later texts the staff burgeons. No doubt this indicates the

miracles which supposedly occurred during the flight into Egypt and the childhood of Jesus. The whole is marked by much coarseness, even by some vulgarisms, and is the expression of a cast of thought which lacks cultural maturity.

Much later, no doubt in the Carolingian era, there appeared a little book called *The Gospel of Mary's Nativity*. This adds nothing to earlier texts, and as a matter of fact, shows the good taste and tact which moved its editor to suppress much of what is so exaggerated and unpleasant in the *Protevangelium Jacobi* and in *Pseudo-Matthew*. As Variot points out, the result is a little book of ten chapters "far superior in taste, moderation, and structure to all writings of this type concerned with the family of Our Lord." It is actually an orthodox revision of older works, one which avoids anything likely to shock the reader.[3] This work was also ascribed to Saint Jerome; and Erasmus, in his edition of that Father's works, accepted the ascription. This *Gospel of the Nativity of Mary* was very well received: Jacobus de Voragine transcribed almost the whole of it in his *Golden Legend*, and to this fact it owes the great influence which apocryphal ideas cast over the artists of the Middle Ages.[4]

---

influence of the Biblical verses, with their Messianic symbolism, *And there shall come forth a rod out of the root of Jesse, and a flower shall rise up out of his root* (Isa. XI; 1), or it may be that here is to be detected the influence of later legendary lore, as for example, the tale of Saint Christopher whose staff is said to have flowered when he took the Infant Jesus on his shoulders. Some of the later manuscripts speak of the anger of the rejected candidates and tell us that one of them, in his chagrin, betook himself to Mount Carmel and became a monk.

[3] Some details are set right, very likely according to sources which reflect the personal knowledge of the writer of this "gospel." Thus the high priest is called Issachar and not, as formerly, Abiathar or Ruben. The birth of Mary takes place at Nazareth rather than at Bethlehem, although that is the original home of her mother's family.

[4] In selecting the texts which appear in the second part of this work, I have preferred to quote from the *Protevangelium Jacobi* and from *Pseudo-Matthew* rather than from this expurgated and later version of the story.

Principal interest is centered upon Mary in this first group
of writings, but in some other works it is only by oblique
references or from situations in which others occupy chief
place in the scene that we are able to discern and to glean
some information about her. It is in a great variety of documents that we find allusions made to her.

We may glance for this purpose at the curious account of
the Nativity which is given in *The Ascension of Isaiah,* a text
to which reference has already been made in what has been
said of the altar screen in the Church of the Madeleine at
Aix-en-Provence. This is an apocryphal work which falls into
the category of those pseudo-apocalypses which flourished to
so great an extent in the first centuries of this era among Jews
and Christians alike. In it the great Prophet of Israel is pictured as having gone up to heaven and, after outrunning time
and the course of history, gazing into the future to behold not
only the earthly life of Christ but his final coming in judgment as well. This work is not lacking beauty in some of its
passages and it has been made use of, either expressly or
allusively, by more than one of the Church Fathers or early
Christian writers, such as Justin, Tertullian and Origen. An
especially favored citation is the portion telling of the martyr-
dom of Isaiah, sawed into two parts. The account of the
Nativity of Our Lord is quite unsatisfactory from the dogmatic point of view, as it implies that the Child did not issue
from the body of his Mother, but was carried down from
heaven. This account is undoubtedly ancient, and it reflects
very well one of the earliest aberrations of early Christianity,
the notion of the Docetists who denied the real nature of the
Incarnation and held the body of Jesus to be a mere
phantasm. *The Ascension of Isaiah* had passed out of notice

for a long time; but the text was recovered in Ethiopia in the early years of the last century.

The various Infancy Gospels form a group so various that their chief link is their complexity. They aim to gather together the chief legends which attempt to depict the daily life of the Child Jesus. *Pseudo-Matthew* contains much that is undoubtedly derived from a Syriac text of the sixth century, the *Gospel of Thomas,* purporting to give an account of certain miraculous occurrences attributed to the Child Jesus. This *Gospel of Thomas* is a quite unpleasant production in which the Infant Saviour is pictured as a frightful urchin, capricious, unaccountable, and sometimes even heartlessly cruel. Mary's place in this production is a very small one: she is pictured as a mother much wearied by these childish pranks. Less displeasing, and not lacking at times in a degree of beauty which can be laid to a naïvely poetic quality of a popular kind, is the *Arabian Gospel of the Infancy.* This was long known in Arabia only—as its name indicates—and the manuscripts date from the twelfth century. Apparently, they are the result of an effort made sometime about the sixth century to gather together all the fabled traditions which had become current in respect to Our Lord's Childhood, and about what had occurred during the flight into Egypt and during the time spent there by the Holy Family, as well as while they lived at Nazareth. A great number of versions existed, some adapted and some revised. The text acquired some new elements as a result of Armenian and Persian influences. This is particularly to be noted in the emphasis laid upon the Magi. It should be pointed out that in all the varying forms taken by this apocryphal work, the role assigned to Our Lady is one wholly appropriate to her. It is perfectly consistent with the most orthodox requirements of faith for it exhibits her as being the great mediatrix of the graces granted by her Divine Son.

The *Gospel of Nicodemus* is perhaps the best known of all the apocryphal books. In the early Church it was more frequently cited than any of the others. It is a delight to delve into it for information about Mary. The text, which seems to be of Greek origin, and which dates probably from the earliest days of Christianity, is full of exceedingly precious details, some of which are in agreement with completely orthodox traditions. The words, *he descended into hell,* of the Apostles' Creed are developed in the second part of this document which is quite admirable. It would seem that many an incident which is called to mind in the Way of the Cross —for example, the episode of Veronica's Veil—seems to be derived from the first part of this gospel, known as the *Acts of Pilate.* However, Our Lady is scarcely mentioned at all in some of the ancient recensions, for instance, that of Abbé Migne in his *Dictionnaire d'Apocryphes.* The editor of this apocryphal work respected the reticence shown by Saint John when he depicted Mary on Calvary. It is only in the more recent revisions, dating from the tenth or eleventh century, that emphasis is laid on the great sorrow and mental anguish of Mary. She is shown bowed in grief, weeping and crying aloud between spasms of sobbing. It was these traditions which influenced the artists of the Middle Ages when they sought to depict Mary in her compassion—her suffering in union with her Son.

The *History of Joseph the Carpenter* contains an account, in its first part, of the death of Our Lord's foster father, supposedly addressed to his disciples by Jesus himself, and the same document depicts Mary at the deathbed of her spouse. It seems that this text dates from the end of the fourth or the beginning of the fifth century and that it originated among the Christians of Egypt. There are fragments of it in Coptic and Arabian versions. The most curious part of this work shows us the soul of Joseph being carried into heaven while his body remains on earth, incorrupt, to await the return of Christ in glory. From this detail we may gather that at the time this book was drawn up, the traditional belief in the Assumption of Our Lady was already established and was thus made an object of imitation.

We shall have to go to the apocryphal documents grouped under the common title of the *Passing of Mary* if we seek to read of the Assumption of Our Lady. There is an extant work dating from the first centuries of Christianity called *Transitus Sanctae Mariae* or the *Passing of Holy Mary* which must have been very well known because the list of apocrypha in the decree of Pope Gelasius makes mention of it. Its age is disputed, some placing it in the third or even in the second century, but the truth of the matter is that the date cannot be exactly determined. The document comes to us in varying guises: there are Syriac, Greek, and Latin versions, all of different length. It is quite impossible to tell whether the Latin version or the Greek one is the older. Père Jugie, the leading specialist on matters having to do with the Assumption, is of the opinion that the various writings called *Transitus Sanctae Mariae* are, in their written form, "no older than the final years of the fifth century." The two chief versions are an Arabic text, extremely prolix and detailed (of which we have a Latin translation as well) and a version, restrained and shorter, known as *Pseudo-Melito*. Although attributed to Melito, the second century bishop of Sardes, it seems rather that this is a re-casting of a book put together in the fifth century by some judicious editor who wished to provide a

[69]

version pruned of exaggerations. In his *Tract on Miracles,* Gregory of Tours has reproduced this work in a form which is not precisely identical with that we ordinarily read, but derives rather from an original in Syriac. It appears that a similar version, ascribed to Saint Jerome, was read in medieval times on the feast of the Assumption. This is also the source from which Jacobus de Voragine drew the main lines of the story as he tells it. For the matter of that, these apocryphal writings known as the *Passing of Mary* were never actually condemned, even though it was known that they actually formed no part of the canonical Scriptures.[5] Although John Damascene, the great Marian theologian who was attached as a Preacher to the Church of the Holy Sepulchre at Jerusalem about 730 A.D., was very severe in his attitude toward the Apocrypha, he nevertheless cites as worthy of credence the report chronicled by the *Transitus* that the Apostles were miraculously recalled to Palestine from the diverse places of their missionary activity in order that they might be present at the deathbed of the Holy Virgin. The development of fundamental theological data—which is, as we shall see, of such great importance in our knowledge of Mary—is here at one with certain information to be gleaned from the Apocrypha. This is not the only such case, and although the employment in theological argumentation of these texts is something which demands much prudence, there is no reason to think that they should be passed over in silence.

[5] In his standard work on Patrology, Père Cayré remarks of the *Transitus:* "This work exerted wide influence: it is wholly orthodox, and there is no reason to think that it represents a Catholic attempt to re-work or edit an heretical original."

TRUTH AND FALSEHOOD IN THE APOCRYPHA

IN RESPECT TO THESE UNUSUAL BOOKS, which are sometimes so sundered from orthodox faith and at other times very closely aligned to it, we are faced with a problem of whether we should give any credence whatever to them or reject them entirely. In order to resolve this difficulty we would have to know when and how these writings came to be and this is something about which we can have very little assurance. An attempt may be made to take into account the underlying intention which seems to have guided the development of these works.

It is easy to discern the psychological motive which served both to inspire these works and to render them popular—it is curiosity, that desire to know which men in general feel in respect to public figures and bearers of great names, and it is a curiosity which is partly legitimate and partly unhealthy. It has been well said that gossip flows as naturally about the great as little vessels throng near a larger ship. The characters who figure in the Gospel narrative are far from being the only people of whom this is true. As a matter of fact, the Gospel itself seems to lend encouragement to this sort of thing. What else is to be drawn from its very last lines in which Saint John says: "But there are also many others things which Jesus did, which if they were written every one, the world itself (I think) would not contain the books to be written"? Does not this seem to authorize the attempt to fill out the lines of the Gospel and to complete it when it fails to give information on precise points? How many are the questions which are in the mind of the reader of the four Gospels, questions to which the text offers no solution? Who is that Zachary of whom Jesus speaks as having been slain between the vestibule and the altar? Who, precisely, are the people who are called "the brethren" of Jesus? Why is the end of the two thieves so very different? As far as Mary is concerned, the names of her parents, the incidents of her married life, her part in the education of Jesus, and a thousand other matters are in question. It is easy to understand the success with which the "revelations" of Saint Bridget of Sweden, Maria d'Agreda, and Sister Katherine Emmerich were received when we consider how in them the whole current of popular fancy was allowed to run riot in order to supply details lacking in the Gospels.

Yet this is not to suggest that the creative imagination was always exercised in a fashion absolutely uncontrolled. It is more than probable that as a basis of these texts there already existed some traditions which were later deformed by overheated fancy. The detail of the grotto of the Nativity, for which the Apocrypha are our only source, may well be an example of something which could have been handed down through a valid tradition. If Saint Justin Martyr, the second century apologist, refers to the grotto, as we have seen in his discussion with Trypho Judæus and speaks of it as a certainty, the matter seems important. He himself was, after all, a native of Palestine, and we may reasonably conclude that he was not deceived on the subject. It is likewise with the detail of the fountain as the scene of the Annunciation, for the memory of this could have lingered on at Nazareth.

Yet there is another psychological element which may have exerted some influence here, and it is one whose importance should not be underestimated. We are dealing with a people —the Jews—who were thoroughly imbued with the sacred writings, in a society of the Primitive Church passionately attached to Holy Scripture, dominated by Biblical influences, and desirous of making the facts of history agree with passages in the Bible which bore the marks of prophecy. When, for example, they read in the Greek version of the Septuagint this verse of Isaiah: "he will dwell in the grotto hollowed from the rock" (XXXIII; 16),[1] would it not seem that these words lent force to belief in the grotto as the place of the Nativity? Would it not appear, as well, that that charming picture of the encounter between Rebecca and the servant of Abraham who had been sent by the Patriarch to seek a wife for his son Isaac and who had found Rebecca marked by grace and by gentleness near the fountain, would mysteriously confirm the fountain as the scene of the Annunciation? Does not Mary's sojourn in the Temple, described in the Apocrypha, awaken an echo of that verse in Ecclesiasticus which the festal liturgy now appropriates to the Holy Virgin: "I have sojourned in the presence of the Lord, in his holy tem-

---

[1] The Hebrew and the Latin text of the Vulgate read: "on the heights"; [the Authorized Version, "on high," with the gloss: "Heb. *heights* or *high places*"; and the Reims-Douay: "He shall dwell on high, the fortifications of rocks shall be his highness."—A.G.]

ple: my dwelling has been in Zion." [2] There are a number of other examples of this sort of analogical thought. It is a kind of thinking which should not be indulged in without restraints for if systematically applied to the Scripture it would reduce their interpretation to the level of a kind of servile matching of texts. It is valuable chiefly as showing an inclination or tendency which may well be among those which mark the Apocrypha as having gathered up some trustworthy data.

Any attempt to form a judgment about the value of the Apocrypha must therefore take into account infinitely complex data. It is for this reason that discussion of them has waxed so furious. The enemies of Christianity have very often used them as artillery in their war against Faith. Thus, Voltaire was fond of repeating that they were documents of capital importance, closer to true traditions than the canonical writings themselves, and that in the beginning it was the Apocrypha alone that the Church recognized as authentic! As a matter of fact, of course, the Church looked upon these books with great distrust from their first appearance. We have already seen that more than one of the Popes and Fathers of the Church judged them severely. Saint Jerome spoke about them in characteristic fashion: he categorically alluded in his rough way to "the mad dreams of the Apocrypha"—*deliramenta Apocryphorum*. Both Saint Jerome and Saint Augustine show themselves full of caution in their attitude toward these writings even when it is a question of points on which the Church has accepted a tradition also known to the Apocrypha, as in the case of identifying Mary's parents. We have seen above how the publication of the *Protevangelium* by Guillaume Postel provoked strong disapproval on the part of

[2] The presence of the ass and the ox by the Crib of the Nativity has a similar origin, being linked to fanciful interpretations of the texts.

Henri Estienne. Of all recent opinions of the Apocrypha the most severe which could be cited is that of Renan. In his introduction to the famous *Vie de Jésus* he calls them "mean and childish wanderings"; and in *L'Église chrétienne,* he writes: "To put these insipid writings on the same level as the masterpieces of Mark, Luke, or Matthew is to demean Christian literature . . . It would be impossible to think of anything more shabby and mean than the Apocrypha. They are full of the tiresome wordiness of an old gossip; their tone is marked by the low familiarity of language characteristic of the nursery."

It must be confessed freely that often—very often, indeed— the Apocrypha deserve these evaluations. Very frequently, childishness and bad taste vie with one another for the ascendency; and often enough immoderation yields only to positive and unadorned stupidity. The most striking thing about all these texts is the note of excess which marks them. They wish to prove too much, and they pile Pelion upon Ossa. The personality of the Virgin Mary is, in this respect, less outrageously treated than others, and the characteristics that have been engrafted upon her by the compilers of the Apocrypha are as nothing by the side of what they have done in obscuring the figure of the Child Jesus. One cannot refrain from shrugging one's shoulders as one reads of the pretended wonders and "miracles" ascribed to this God whom they have turned into an urchin; and it is with a sense of embarrassed discomfort that one notes the spirit of revenge shown against his little playmates, the mockery which he turns upon the schoolmasters, against whom he rebels, and the open contempt which he displays for his foster father.

In the Apocrypha there are also a number of scenes in which Our Lady figures which are frankly shocking. For

[75]

example, the Sanhedrin is made to decree that she is to be
subjected to the ordeal of the "bitter waters" in order to determine if the conception of her child were adulterous.
Even more shocking is the well-known episode in which a
midwife demands a physiological proof of the virginity of
Our Lady. What strikes the reader most forcibly in going over
the Apocrypha as a whole is their complete lack of humility:
the authentic evangelists freely avowed that they did not know
everything, they felt many important matters under the shade
of the mysterious unknown, but the pseudo-evangelists pre-
tend to know all and to tell all. What the result of their in-
ventiveness is, we have seen.

Despite all this, it cannot be said that the Apocrypha are
no more than a constant statement of perverse leanings. This
would be no more true of them than it is of *The Arabian
Nights' Entertainment.* Nevertheless, it is not to be denied
that among them there are writings of evil intent which
sought by employing evident exaggeration to implant heretical ideas. Saint Irenæus, in his day, had pointed out that it
is a property of the sectarian mind to bring forth books
designed to deceive the simple and to lead astray those whose
faith is weak. And Origen noted that "Although the Church
has no more than four Gospels, heresy has a much greater
number." The Docetists, who denied the Incarnation, had
influenced the accounts like the one which disfigures the
Ascension of Isaiah, in which the Infant Jesus is made to
appear all at once by the side of Mary without there being
question of any process of being born in the natural fashion of human beings. It may well be that the origin of some
of the fabulous details which have been woven about the
childhood of Our Lord is to be sought in the whirlpool of
Gnostic ideas. Yet, where Mary is concerned, it seems that

[76]

there were but few sources of influence upon the apocryphal texts which inclined them to present her in an unbecoming way.

Having made these reservations—and it is well that we begin with them—we ought by no means stop at them. Not all is untrue in these false gospels, not everything they offer is worthy of being rejected, and we must even pause to emphasize the fact that the apocryphal writings played a useful part in the intellectual development of the first Christians.

In the first place the apocryphal gospels are evidence in favor of the Canonical Gospels, inasmuch as every counterfeit necessarily stems from an authentic model. Tertullian has pointed out that "Truth must exist in order to be falsified." The compilers of the Apocrypha accepted without question the whole framework of the Gospels as we know it. The characters with whom they people their books are the very same as those whose names we read in the Gospel and very often the way in which they develop their theme is no more than a gloss upon what we find in the New Testament. In many other cases they borrow from it *ad litteram*. The apocryphal gospel may, in fact, be compared to the historical novel, for the perspective of each is quite similar. The facts of history can serve as a foundation for the elaborations of the imaginative writer only on condition that the general trend of factual matter, which is common knowledge, be not destroyed. Similarly, if the Apocrypha were to be acceptable, they would have to be based upon facts generally known to Christians. It follows that at the time that these imaginative works were produced the basic narrative found in the Gospels must have been generally held to be true.

Yet this is not the only positive element which we must allow that they possess. It is no more than fair to admit that

[77]

in the midst of a great mass of rubbish there are to be found not only some particles of gold dust but even some nuggets of pure gold. Thus it happens that there often arises from these otherwise tiresome narratives, despite the lack of taste which sometimes disfigures them, a certain mysterious charm which wins the reader inexplicably, just as does the *Golden Legend* of the Middle Ages. It is this strange charm which subdued the artists of the Romanic and Gothic periods. One cannot fail to respond to the smiling tenderness with which *Pseudo-Matthew* and the *Protevangelium* recount the daily life of the child Mary, picturing her as a grave little housewife of only three, already serious in mien and overshadowed by Divine Grace. Nor can the account of the suitors with their staves and the mysterious designation of Joseph be considered as wanting in charm. And surely a breath of real greatness stirs through the pages in which the Apocrypha, in describing Our Lord's birth, picture all Nature at rest and stilled in wonder, as though the movement of time itself had been brought suddenly to a stop by a happening so stupendous in import. And some majesty must be allowed to those long descriptions of the "Magi Kings" which in their varying versions the *Gospels of the Infancy* so abundantly offer. There are times when they even convey a profoundly meaningful thought. When they show us the wild beasts who adore the Infant God as he passes through the desert on the flight into Egypt, are they not symbolizing the fact that all things made owe their submission to God by the mere act of existing? When Mary foresees two nations, one marked by happiness and the other by desperation, is not this a kind of Pauline commentary on the drama of Israel or at least a good theological outline of the "two paths," one leading to salva-

[78]

tion and the other to rejection, a concept which the Fathers of the Church loved to dwell upon? [3]

How often it is that these beautiful ideas are based upon lively faith and devotion. One finds passages in the Apocrypha where the soul's joy is expressed in a most worthy and authentic way. Such is the hymn in which Saint Anne bewails her barrenness and begs the Lord to have pity upon her: in its words one breathes a climate entirely appropriate to Holy Writ. So is it also with the explanation given by the Angel to Mary concerning the mystery to be accomplished in her. Here again the tone is exactly as it should be. And, it need not be remarked, the compilers of the various accounts of the *Passing of Mary* were animated only by a tender devotion and by a wish to make known the undeniable glorification of God's Mother as manifested in the miracle of her Assumption.

Even some of what seem to us quite shocking notes of the Apocryphal writings were the result of well-meaning effort. An incident in point is the account of the midwife. When the *Protevangelium Jacobi* began to circulate in the second century, the question which was agitating the Christian community was that which Trypho Judæus ironically put to Saint Justin Martyr: "Tell me how in heaven's name it can be that a man can be born of a virgin?" The anti-Christian controversialist, Celsus, declared that Jesus was no more than the son of a working-woman of Judea. It was in order to answer such attacks that the compilers of the Apocrypha forged such tales as those of the "bitter waters" and the midwife. The consequence may justly provoke the well-known hope that one be saved from one's friends, but there can be no question that the purpose of these writers was

3 All the texts alluded to here will be found in Part I.

well-intentioned. The guiding principle they had in view was the vindication of Mary's virginity. In order to prove this, recourse was had to methods of demonstration which concentrated on minutiae in the manner of Judaic legalism, and the inevitable, though unwished-for result, is shocking to our eyes.

There are worthwhile dogmatic data to be found in the Apocrypha even if they are passed over in silence by the Canonical Scriptures. It is the former which record the descent of Our Lord into Hell, of which mention has already been made; and in reference to Our Lady, the great events of her Presentation in the Temple and of her Assumption are chronicled in the Apocrypha. In many of the Oriental Churches certain extracts from the Apocrypha were used on various occasions, as the feasts of Saints Anne and Joachim. An apocryphal work is not necessarily and ineluctably the just object of condemnatory decrees. There can be no justification for regarding with excessive severity traditions which have flowered and gained currency in the imagination of faithful Christian people. It is enough that the Church show herself prudent in accepting them officially, and this she has done. Although these works are not wholly true, elements and scraps of truth are to be seen in them. The problem arises as to how these varied elements are to be recognized for what they actually are.

It is in this regard that care must be taken to avoid a mistake even more serious than that which is made by those who totally reject the Apocrypha and who think that the mere fact that an incident is reported in them is sufficient to stamp it as false. They also are mistaken who think, on the contrary, that in the Apocrypha are the *sources* of Christian dogma and institutions. According to the learned Sulpician, Abbé Le

Hir, "This is the most widely believed illusion, common to critics of the Rationalist or Protestant school. Our most ancient devotions to Our Lady, many of her festivals, well-established pious beliefs, such as that in her corporeal Assumption,[4] even the solemnly defined dogma of her Immaculate Conception—all these, according to such critics, have no foundation other than their presence in the Apocryphal writings." The truth of the matter is entirely different: it can only be comprehended in the light of an understanding of the gradual unfolding of devotion to Mary, of the penetration into and development of dogma as being part of the Church's deposit of faith from the very beginning, as something in which Tradition has played a formative role. The Apocrypha, which are popular accounts of deeply seated beliefs held by Christians from early times, have indubitably gathered together elements which are outside the ordered currents of orthodox piety, but these elements do not constitute the essential points in these texts. It is from the standpoint and before the bar of authentic tradition that the Apocrypha are to be judged. It is not they which are to be regarded as a measuring-stick against which the value of tradition is to be summarily estimated.

4 [Le Hir wrote, of course, before the dogmatic definition in the apostolic constitution of Pope Pius XII, "Munificentissimus Deus" (*Acta Apostolicae Sedis*, XLII; 753-73; November 4, 1953), declaring the Assumption of the Virgin to be an article of Catholic faith.—A.G.]

TEN

MARY IN THE EARLY CHURCH

RECOURSE THEREFORE MUST BE HAD to the tradition of the Church. This is to be done not in order to seek therein for confirmation of some of the data of the Apocrypha, but rather in an effort to understand how the figure of Mary has gradually emerged from the shadows which conceal her in the Gospel narrative into that brilliant light in which we see her today. An entire body of data must be taken into consideration, data linked in the deepest sense to the historical growth of early Christianity, and developed according to the dictates of a logic so compelling that it cannot be termed other than Providential.

One point is established and it is one admitted by every historian of the Primitive Church: in early Christian worship the place accorded to Mary is quite small. One cannot say that she was overlooked in the devotional life of Christians, but on the whole she did not, in any sense, occupy the place she holds today. Up until at least the fourth century, there seems to have been no actual Marian liturgy, and it would be quite true to say that her memory was kept on no more than one or two feasts. Very few churches were dedicated in her honor; they were certainly less numerous than those placed under the invocation of one or another of the apostles or martyrs. It almost seems that the early Christians were so astonished and as it were dazzled by the greatest of the mysteries of religion, the Incarnation, the Redemption, and the Resurrection, that they were unable to concentrate their attention upon any of the less evident certitudes of faith, or upon a figure who had been cast into the shadow because she was so close to the glorious light which marked the person of the Christ.

This rudimentary nature of devotion to Mary, which seems so surprising to some observers is, nevertheless, to be regarded as being wholly consonant with the picture of the Virgin's personality presented to us in the Gospel. Cardinal Newman expressed this very well indeed when he wrote in some remarks on devotion to Our Lady in the Catholic Church: "You know, when first He went out to preach, she kept apart from Him; she interfered not in His work; and even when He was gone up on high, yet she, a woman, went not out to preach or teach, she seated not herself in the Apostolic Chair, she took no part in the priest's office . . . Nor when she . . . had left this lower scene, and she was a Queen upon her Son's right hand, not even then did she ask of Him to publish her name to the ends of the world, or to hold her up to the world's gaze, but she remained waiting for the time, when her own glory should be necessary for His." [1]

The concluding words of this passage express perfectly the way in which primitive Christians were, in a sense, *obliged* to picture Mary. As a matter of fact, doctrinal reasons im-

[1] J. H. Newman: Discourse XVII: "The Glories of Mary for the Sake of Her Son"; *Discourses Addressed to Mixed Congregations* (London: © Longmans, Green & Co., 1929); pp. 356-357.

pelled the faithful of the early ages to speak of God's Virgin Mother. It was only a short while after its beginnings that Christianity was attacked by that disease of mind and soul which is called heresy. The earliest of the heresies were concerned with the person of Our Lord. That sacred person was the object and the showing forth of the deepest of all mysteries, of those which human reason found most repugnant to itself; because of this it was the person of Christ that was most heatedly discussed from the inception of the Christian era.

One group of heretical thinkers, the Docetists, maintained that Christ had assumed only the appearance of human nature (*dokein* in Greek means *to appear*). They held that his body was no more than a phantasm, a heavenly body manifested to men but one entirely unlike their own bodies of human flesh and blood. In the Gnostic heresies we encounter similar concepts to the effect that Our Lord was no more than a kind of metaphysical link between God and man, an *eon* or emanation of the divine Power. Similar aberrations marked contrary vagaries of human thought and went by varying names: *adoptionism, sabellianism,* and the like, all of which seem to have joined forces in the formidable movement called *Arianism,* which saw Jesus as no more than a man, confessedly unique, but only a man, one who had become divine by a kind of promotion accorded him in deference to his merits.

Now the antidote for both these perversions of a true Christology is found in the simple act of belief in Mary, the Virgin Mother of Jesus. To declare that Mary had actually and truly brought Jesus into the world established the humanity of her child, as against the teaching of the Docetists, while belief that his birth was of a Virgin Mother sufficed to

[84]

profess the transcendental nature of him who became man in a way unlike that common to mankind. It is for this reason that the opening chapters of the Gospel according to Saint Luke are of capital importance; for this were they attacked by the enemies of Christianity and for this were they defended by the Church Fathers. For the same reason, in the first summaries of Christian doctrine which the catechumens were required to recite as a requisite for their admission into the Church, in those credal formularies which Tertullian called the *Canons of the Faith,* and which the familiar *Apostles' Creed* preserves for us almost word for word,[2] it was proclaimed that *Jesus Christ was born of the Virgin Mary.* "Hear not those who will not confess that Jesus Christ, the son of David, was born of the Virgin Mary!" In this precept of the great Martyr of Antioch, Saint Ignatius, is summed up what the whole Church says to her children in telling them that the virginity of Mary is, as it were, the safeguard of the Faith.[3]

In the light of our knowledge of Mary, which is now the subject of our consideration, these assertions of dogmatic truths were the cause of Christians acquiring better understanding of two basic notes of her character: her divine maternity and her virginity. When the earliest Church Fathers speak of Mary it is usually to discuss these qualities in her.

Saint Ignatius of Antioch, Saint Justin, and in their wake

---

[2] Cf. the author's *L'Église des Apôtres et Martyrs,* chapter V, in which a paragraph is devoted to this point. The Creed of Nicea of 325 did not name Mary in its first version but it was completed in 381 at Constantinople. This later version became our solemn Creed which is used at the Eucharist (cf. chapter XI of the work cited). [And see also the notes and references therein indicated in H. Daniel-Rops: *This Is the Mass;* translated by Alastair Guinan (New York: © Hawthorn Books, 1958); p. 150; note (1) to Ch. X.—A.G.]

[3] There have already been cited a number of equally categorical statements of this principle.

many another, affirm that Mary actually brought God into the world, that she is "the Mother of God," *theotokos*—the God bearer; but it may be asked what can they mean by the assertion that she, a mortal woman, is "the Mother of God." The question arose naturally, and consideration had to be given to it. Saint Irenæus was able to show the underlying relationship which links her privilege of motherhood to the mission of our Lord; and in the third century, the Alexandrian Pierius preached a full discourse on this theme of the divine Maternity about the year 280 A.D., while the great Saint Epiphanius of Palestine devoted himself to elucidating it in the century following.

The other of Mary's chief qualities, her virginity, the notion of a virgin conceiving a child, of a virgin giving birth to one, was heatedly discussed. Tertullian, the doughty African controversialist, beset by the necessity of combating the Docetists who held that Jesus was never truly born in the flesh, had maintained Mary's virginity only in the conception of Jesus, and relinquished it in and after her act of actually giving birth to her Son. Later on Bonosius and the Arian Helvidius were persuaded that Mary had other children after the birth of Jesus. But almost all the Fathers ranged themselves against this opinion, which their consensus adjudged to be blasphemous. They found its refutation in the figure of Mary as the Gospel shows her to us, and in the tradition of the Church. The mystery of Mary can be understood only in the light of her perpetual virginity, a virginity enduring before, during, and after the birth of Jesus. It is this perpetual virginity that lends the figure of Mary the spiritual greatness which was seen, little by little, to set her apart. All this is to be gleaned from the Marian writings of Saint Ignatius, Saint

Justin, Saint Irenæus, Clement of Alexandria,[4] Saint Ephrem, Saint Epiphanius, and later on Saint Ambrose and Saint Jerome in their respective refutations of Bonosius and Helvidius.

It may be stated that at the end of the fourth century Mary's two fundamental characteristics, her divine maternity and her perpetual virginity were part of accepted doctrine.

There was another element in primitive Christianity which helped toward an understanding of the character of Mary, and this was the intense interest which was felt in the Sacred Scripture. The New Testament, which was certainly established canonically about the middle of the second century, was held in fervent regard, as is evidenced not only by the writings of the Fathers but in the Acts of the Martyrs as well. Passages from it were publicly read during Mass, and at home they would be re-read and made the subject of meditation. Naturally, therefore, even the slightest details of the text would be earnestly scrutinized, and all the characters mentioned—especially she who gave life to Jesus—would be the objects of deep interest. It would be impossible to reflect upon the Gospel text and yet fail to encounter the mysterious figure of Mary.

[4] It is undoubtedly Clement of Alexandria who exhibits the deepest understanding of the spiritual implications of Mary's virginity, as is shown by his meaningful words: "The fruitful virginity of Mary is comparable to that of the written Word of the Lord. The Holy Scriptures are fruitful by reason of the light which shines from them and the truth which they bring into the world; but they nevertheless remain virginal as they enclose, in a pure and holy vessel, the mysteries of Truth." This transcendant similarity between Mary and the Gospel has been pictured in sacred art as, for example, in the miniature of *Our Lady dictating the Gospel* of the *Codex purpureus,* a seventh century manuscript in the Cathedral of Rossano. The miniature may be interpreted in two ways: it may be a representation of the traditional belief that Saint Luke drew his inspiration directly from the Holy Virgin for the opening chapters of his Gospel, or it may refer to what was a favorite idea with several Fathers of the Church and was so well expressed by Clement of Alexandria in the passage quoted above.

[87]

Nor is this all. The primitive Christians, especially the early Fathers of the Church, were thoroughly imbued with the old Hebraic learning and took a deep interest in the books of the Old Law. To their study they applied a method which had far-reaching results. Like Philo Judæus of Alexandria, whose method they Christianized, they looked in the words of the Old Testament for whatever seemed to foreshadow, announce, or prefigure the New Dispensation. This method of exegesis is termed figurative or *typological* and the richness of association and analogy which it evokes has awakened innumerable echoes in the liturgy, in art, and in poetry; and by these means it still exerts considerable influence upon Christian thought. Its underlying principle suggests that Sacred Scripture, in addition to its literal meaning, contains, particularly since it is the expression of divine ideas and is inspired by God, another meaning even more penetrating, that is to say the spiritual or prophetic sense. Did not Christ himself make use of this method when he used the dramatic incident of Jonah, swallowed by the whale and then expelled by that monster, as a type or prophecy of the Resurrection? Similarly, does not the water which Moses caused to flow from the rock on Horeb signify and prefigure that "living water" promised by Jesus to the Samaritan woman? Is not the manna in the desert, a kind of miraculous food which was indefinitely renewed, a type or figure of the Eucharist?

If it be read with this notion in mind, Scripture is full of ideas which are readily applied to Mary. To begin with, it is evidently she to whom reference is made in the well-known verse where Isaiah (VII; 14) according to the Greek version, declares: "A Virgin shall conceive and bear a Son." And may not all the graces and virtues of the chosen bride in the *Song of Songs* be rightly appropriated to her? Is not the same legitimately done with the notes typical of wisdom of which we read in Proverbs (VIII), in Ecclesiasticus (XXIV), or throughout the whole of the book which itself bears the title of Wisdom?

There is in Holy Writ another character who appears to be strangely linked to Mary, not in the sense that she prefigures her but rather that she is her opposite, one whose existence made necessary the coming of Mary just as night must be followed by day: this is Eve, the woman who sinned and caused the fall of man. In Chapter III of Genesis (13-16), following closely the reproaches of God to Eve for her disobedience, do we not also find a promise of victory, which later is to be won by a woman over the serpent whose head it is said she will crush? Mary comes forth as the woman appointed to win this victory—a victory over sin. In the light of this line of thought, the quite modest role which she plays in the Gospel appears to be one of the greatest importance. The drama of humankind thus becomes intertwined with an economy of supernatural revenge—the revenge of man upon the Demon—and of this revenge Mary, by bringing Jesus into the world, is the instrument.

Was Saint John thinking of the Holy Church or of the Holy Virgin when in the great twelfth chapter of the Apocalypse he depicted the woman "clothed in the sun and crowned with twelve stars" against whom the dragon of evil wages a dreadful battle? It may be that these concepts merge. At any rate, as early as the second century, the Fathers had very plainly expressed the parallelism which has become traditional in the Church: Mary is the "new Eve," destined by her purity to blot out the sin of the first mother of mankind, and by her obedience destined to ransom the children of the disobedient first parents of humanity. In his dialogue

[89]

with Trypho Judæus, Saint Justin states this explicitly and Saint Irenæus also takes up the idea when he writes: "The chains forged by Eve's disobedience restrain us until they are broken by Mary's obedience. What the virgin Eve bound by her infidelity, the Virgin Mary has set free by her trust in God."

To the consideration of Mary's role in Scripture were added a host of moral and psychological considerations. Because of its prime importance, the part of Mary was subjected to the strictest analysis. In order that she might blot out the fault of the first woman, Mary, the "new Eve," was clothed with all possible perfection. But is not this precisely the way Mary appears in the Gospel where she is portrayed as the model of all, a woman vested with every virtue in its highest degree? To the extent that the fullness of Christianity is given practical expression in life and to the degree that the study of the words of the Gospel is most profound, Mary is revealed, ever more clearly, in the fullness of her perfection as an example to all. The Fathers, certainly from the fourth century on, made her holiness the theme of their writings: it is Mary whom Saint Ambrose holds up for imitation by young girls and by women and he does this in pages marked by charming delicacy of thought and expression. Saint Augustine declares that such a being as Mary must be entirely untouched by sin and in this notion psychological analysis and dogmatic affirmation are at one, for it is thus that the wonderful character of the Holy Virgin, revealed in the essence of her being, becomes clear to our minds.

We have been concerned, in our quest for the historic Mary, with a consideration of the attitude manifested by primitive Christianity in two of its most vital aspects, the formulation of dogmatic principle and the interpretation and

[90]

use of Holy Scripture. But we must consider another aspect of early Christianity as well: it is a movement, much freer and much less regulated, seen in the currents of popular piety and devotion which develop under the leading of the others. We know relatively little about this aspect of Christian life but we may pick out its various sources. The mere act of reading the Gospel account of Our Lord's birth given by Saint Luke, is quite enough to draw the devout soul who is meditating upon its words to look upon Mary with love and veneration. In Palestine, moreover, local tradition would keep alive certain associations with Mary—such were the places and houses in which she lived. It is in this area that popular belief plays its main role, for the Apocrypha would naturally preserve in written form the sum of what was commonly thought. The result is as complex and confused as life itself and what we find is a record of a young and growing society, spiritually restless.

Little by little, there appeared in Christianity signs of special devotion to Mary. First there were festivals in her honor specifically directed to the consideration of certain of her qualities, and these were gradually added to the liturgical calendar. So it is that we find the Sunday before Christmas set aside as the *Commemoration of the Virgin Mary.* Her image can be found on the walls of the Catacombs where she is often pictured as a young mother holding her child, the Virgin to whom the prophet Isaiah foretells that she will bear a son. In a subterranean sanctuary in Alexandria which dates from the third century, a fresco represents the Marriage Feast at Cana, and in it the Mother of Christ is seen speaking to the servants. She is specifically identified as *Haghia Maria* or Holy Mary.

By the middle of the fourth century the current of devotion to Mary had begun to rise. Not only theological writers and learned doctors who made use of the figure of Mary in the explanation of Christian belief by extolling her extraordinary virtues, but simple souls, as well, discovered in her the same thing that we love in her today. They recognized in her that tender and loving personality before whom every man feels himself to be her child, that fountain of affectionate help and motherly consolation which showers aid and relief upon us in our need. Thus do we find Saint Gregory of Nyssa writing his *Life of Saint Gregory the Wonderworker* and telling us of the apparitions with which Our Lady favored that holy bishop in Asia Minor. The description of these apparitions, set down so long ago, links them with those that have taken place at Lourdes, at La Salette, at Fatima. Particularly notable among writers is Saint Ephrem, the Mesapotamian mystic, who, living in solitary retreat near Edessa, wrote long poems in praise of Our Lady in which he saluted her in a manner like that we use in prayers of our own, prayers such as those written by Saint Bernard or Saint Grignion de Montfort, by Claudel or by Péguy. "Most Holy Lady, Mother of God, uniquely pure in soul and body, Lady full of grace and of the Holy Spirit, look upon me sinful as I am, stained in body and in soul. Direct my straying thoughts which wander in darkness; rule and govern my feelings; deliver me from the bondage of my sins, so that having cast off the dark chains of evil, I may worthily glorify you." Herein we find the notion of Mary as the Mediatrix, the Advocate of men before the Most High. The concept which is voiced in this prayer is certainly close to that which determined our *Memorare*.

It is particularly after the fifth century that Marian devotion is seen to take large strides forward, surrounding Our

Lady with the very same light in which we are accustomed to view her. At the beginning of that century, Nestorius, bishop of Constantinople, became involved in acrimonius theological disputes and felt called upon to oppose the use of the term *theotokos,* "God-bearer," or "Mother of God" which had won acceptance throughout the Church. His attitude met with universal reprobation and from every side came protests from those who resented opinions derogatory to the high status which had been given to the Holy Virgin. The vehemence of these protests establishes the place which Mary held in the eyes of her devout followers. The most eminent contemporary theologians took part in this dispute and Saint Cyril of Alexandria constituted himself, with impassioned forcefulness, as the champion of Mary and her divine maternity. The entire affair aroused so great a disturbance that it became necessary to convene a General Council, which was held at Ephesus in 431, and there the condemnation of Nestorius was pronounced. As soon as the decision became known, crowds of people thronged about the two hundred bishops who had proclaimed it. They saluted the prelates and carried them in triumph in a torchlit procession during which some women went to the extent of burning incense before the bishops.

This pronouncement of the Church, vindicating the eminent place which is Mary's, was the spur to a current of devotion to her which exceeded even what had hitherto been felt. Congregation after congregation associated itself with the acclamation composed by Saint Cyril to express the triumph of the *theotokos* or "God-bearer." It is a beautiful composition and Bossuet, who was himself most devoted to Mary, later translated it. There now began to be sung hymns in praise of Mary like those of the poet Prudentius or like that apt little composition, *Salve Sancta Parens,* written by

[93]

the priest Cælius Sedulius and preserved by the Roman Missal as the Introit for votive Masses of Our Lady. Those moving tales of Mary's intervention in the history of souls were told and re-told. One is that of Saint Mary of Egypt, a sinful woman whose course of life was changed when she found pardon while praying before an image of the Virgin. The chief Marian festivals were now celebrated and became fixtures in the liturgical calendar: the Annunciation, the Presentation in the Temple,[5] and a little later (about the sixth or seventh century), the Assumption. Representations of Mary were set up with increasing frequency in churches and in other places of prayer, and she began to occupy a place in the panels of mosaics, with which it was then customary to adorn church walls, as well as in sculptured ornamentation then beginning to be used in ecclesiastical architecture. There is one such representation, an evocative picture of Our Lady at prayer in the Temple of Jerusalem, engraved on a tombstone which may be seen at Saint Maximin. She is shown in supplication before the Lord in the attitude of the classical *orantes*.[6]

We, therefore, find that about the sixth or seventh century the currents spurred by the spontaneous inclination of Christian devotion to Mary were joined by the currents which underlay the dogmatic speculations of doctors and theologians. The place of the Holy Virgin in the life of devotion

---

[5] [That is to say, the *Presentation of Our Lord* in the Temple, or Candlemas Day (February 2) which, although reckoned by liturgists as a *festum Domini*, has always been strongly associated with Our Lady because of her central role in the event commemorated. Sometimes, although not with strict correctness, it is called the feast of the *Purification of Mary*. The feast of her own Presentation, November 21, is of much later advent as a liturgical commemoration, as has been pointed out.—A.G.]

[6] This ancient work of art is in the crypt of the Madeleine at Saint-Maximin (Var) and is believed to be the oldest image of Our Lady in France.

had become solidly established in the tradition of the Church in both East and West, and "Mariology" became a recognized branch of theology. This mustard seed planted by the Gospel was to grow into a great tree which, century by century, would take firm root in all Christian lands where it was destined to flower in the diverse fashions which we today know so well.

ELEVEN

THE HEART IN THE
UNDERSTANDING OF DOGMA

I HAVE NO INTENTION of attempting a sketch of the history of devotion to Mary—such an effort would require a long book. How much would have to be included, how many names and titles would have to be cited! There are, first of all, those sublimely prayerful and wondrous hymns which rose up like the best fruits of the soul in the Middle Ages: the *Ave Maris Stella,* the *Regina Coeli,* the *Alma Redemptoris Mater,* the *Salve Regina* so dear to Godefroy de Bouillon's Crusaders, and dear to Saint Bernard as well. There is also the angelical salutation, the *Ave Maria,* whose history is linked to the development of devotion to Our Lady. Pages of meditations, ceaselessly repeated through the ages, recount the grace and virtues of Mary, and the words in which they do so are the words of Saint Anselm, Saint Bernard, Saint Albert the Great, Saint Thomas Aquinas, Saint Bonaventure, Blessed Henry Suso, Saint Francis de Sales, Cardinal de Bérulle, M. Olier, and the great Jacques-Bénigne Bossuet, as well as of a host

[96]

of others. In the roll of poets who have sung her glory, poets from Rutebœuf to Péguy, we find names of varying degrees of fame, among them Arnoul Gréban and Pierre Gringoire, Dante, Camoëns, and Corneille. The great Marian devotion, the Rosary, began obscurely in the eleventh century and was later systematically developed by Saint Dominic and took the form in which we now know it as comprising the recitation of prayer and meditation on the fifteen mysteries, about the time of the Hundred Years' War. Thus briefly passed in review are some indications of that remarkable surge of devotion which sufficed both to assure to the Virgin her high place in Christian worship where she ranks second to Christ himself, and, as well, to make her the object of deep study in order that she and her place in the divine plan might be better understood.

Here we must pause to estimate the force of this spontaneous surge of the soul's devotion and attempt to point out its consequences. It must be confessed that when we turn our thoughts back to the early centuries, to the original manifestations of devotion to Our Lady, although we recognize that the appropriately dogmatic preoccupation of the theologians was to underline certain qualities in Mary's character, nevertheless, the result was a lack of spontaneity one scarcely knows how to describe. The great gift of simplicity of heart seems to have been denied these learned men and they appear never to have discerned the profound attractiveness of Mary's personality in a way that would have allowed them to feel it in all its radiant loveliness. They were indeed awake to all the reasons which move the intellect, but they seem not to have known the reason of the heart. Age after age, it is ever the same, and Père Régamey has well expressed the situation by saying: "Popular devotion is always the source of initiative. The liturgy takes up the theme, and finally the theologians work out explicit statements of Mary's prerogatives, and of the devotion to her which they themselves share."

The question at issue is to determine how great a degree of reliance ought be placed upon this spontaneous devotional surge of the believing soul on this reasoning of the heart. And in this connection, recourse is to be had to that great concept fundamentally fixed in Catholicism, the notion of Tradition, ceaselessly uniting one generation with another, at once fixed and yet developing, just as life itself develops. After Pentecost the Church remains the abode of the Holy Spirit; in her totality she cannot fall into doctrinal error, and whenever a conviction springs forth from the depths of her collective consciousness, whenever this conviction finds expression in prayers officially authorized, the Church cannot do otherwise than confirm what is a revelation of truth. This idea was beautifully expressed as early as the final years of the fourth century when Saint Paulinus of Nola wrote: "Take heed of the pulsation of the hearts of the faithful; for it is in those hearts that the Holy Spirit lives!"

It therefore follows that propositions held as true by the generality of Christians, particularly when they take definite form in prayers, liturgical worship, and devotions authorized by the Church, may be utilized in line with what has been said above of the function of Tradition, whenever theologians seek to find practical proofs of theses which they wish to establish. A document bearing the title *De gratia Dei* (or a *Treatise on God's Grace*), formerly attributed to Pope Celestine I (431), but which appears rather to be a sixth century decretal, explicitly tells us that "attention is to be given to prayers generally in use throughout the Church

[98]

Catholic, in such way that the canon of our belief is established by the canon of our prayer." This is often summed up in the formulary: *lex supplicandi statuit legem credendi,* which is to say that our devotional life illustrates the principles underlying our faith.

It follows that a doctrinal proposition, even if not set forth as infallible by the Sovereign Pontiff or by a Church Council, nevertheless cannot be disregarded by a believer when the almost unanimous opinion of the Church favors that proposition. There is, of course, much latitude permissible in respect to interpreting and explaining it so long as authority fails to pronounce upon the proposition in question; but it cannot be explicitly disregarded or treated or thought of as if it were lacking in warrant. In this sense the *Syllabus* formally condemned the thesis stating that "only those propositions which have been set forth as dogmas of faith to be held by all, according to the infallible judgment of the Church, are alone binding in strict obligation on Catholic teachers and writers." To express this in another way, making use of a concrete example, it may be said that belief in the Assumption of Our Lady, affirmed by the all but unanimous agreement of the faithful and enshrined in the liturgy, could not be rejected by a Catholic even though there is no explicit reference to it in the Canonical Scriptures, even though it were not taught *ex cathedra* by infallible authority; Tradition, in any event, imposes it upon believers.

Although revelation is generally the concomitant of a state of elevation in the soul by which a kind of mystical outrush penetrates by faith to the spontaneous apprehension of truth which is implicit and seemingly hidden, it is, nevertheless, the duty of theologians to supervene and to attempt by definition and analysis to lend precision to the truth re-

[99]

vealed. One of the notes or marks of the Catholic Church which is but ill understood by her adversaries is thus linked to her conception of Tradition as a living and continuous deposit of faith.

The Church regards the *development of Dogma* as not merely legitimate but necessary. For this reason the history of dogmatic belief has become a most significant field for the work of the theologians. We find that Père Lebreton on the history of the dogma of the Trinity, Père Prat on that of the Immaculate Conception, Père Jugie on that of the Assumption, have called attention to principles whose influence cannot be ignored. It is well-known that his own careful studies along these lines led Newman to reject Protestantism and to enter into communion with the Apostolic See.

This notion is essentially two-sided in the same sense that a coin has two sides: one emphasizes stability, the other a continuous development. The Catholic and Roman Church holds that the age of Revelation was closed by the death of the last of the Lord's Apostles, which is to say, that since then there has been no addition to the body of sacred belief which was received by them from Jesus and passed on by them in their function as his faithful witnesses. But the Church has developed the principles and radical ideas which from the beginning were rooted in that body of belief, just as the Apostles did; and she has done this, as the Vatican Council puts it, "in such wise as the conditions of time and circumstance require." To put this idea in another way, it may be said that acting in accord with legitimate Tradition, the Church has neither innovated nor changed anything fundamental; all she has done is to explain, to deepen men's understanding of, and to state more clearly, the content of the deposit of faith. It must be admitted that this is a magnificent conception; for by it the Spirit is seen to effect a perduring illumination of the mind of man. It reveals the pulsation of a life which has for almost two thousand years continuously animated the soul of the Church in order to develop within her those seeds planted by her Lord and destined eventually to expand into a great tree.

Unless the significance of this *dogmatic life* be taken into consideration, unless it be recognized that the Holy Spirit is the spur of this life and that the process of its growth is directed and ruled by Tradition, one cannot have a just idea of the importance which Catholics (and, to some degree, Orthodox Greeks, as well) give to Mary. Nor can one remain in ignorance of certain aspects of her personality as they have been brought into relief. Cardinal Newman expressed this admirably when, in writing to Dr. Pusey on the subject of devotion to Our Lady, he said: "I fully grant that devotion towards the Blessed Virgin has increased among Catholics with the progress of centuries; I do not allow that the doctrine concerning her has undergone a growth, for I believe that it has been in substance one and the same from the beginning." [1]

Should it be desired to analyze certain notes of Mary's character best known to us today, although they are not explicitly mentioned in the Gospel, reference must be made, to be rightly understood, to two concepts, both of which are associated with the historical growth of Christianity. These concepts concern the growth of the life of devotion and the development of dogma. There can be no doubt that our knowledge of Mary owes very much to both of these.

[1] J. H. Newman: "Letter to the Rev. E. B. Pusey"; *Difficulties of Anglicans* (London: Longmans, Green, & Co., 1918); vol. II.

Let us consider the dogma of the Immaculate Conception. As is well known this was defined on December 8, 1854, by Pope Pius IX in the following words of his Encyclical *Ineffabilis Deus:* "We pronounce and declare that the doctrine that the Blessed Virgin Mary was, from the first instant of her Conception, preserved and exempt, by especial grace and privilege of Almighty God foreseeing the merits of Jesus Christ, saviour of the human race, from all taint of original sin, is a doctrine revealed by God and that it consequently must be firmly and unreservedly believed by all the faithful." [2] Here we have not only an important dogmatic definition declaring that a woman, a creature, is exempt from the terms of the universal law which has governed all mankind since the Fall of Adam, but also a most precious piece of information concerning Mary's character and her psychological traits. Now, none of this is based on any New Testament text and wonder arises as to how the Church, speaking through the infallible voice of the Pope, has been led to make this declarations.

The reply is simple. Although the *doctrine* of the Immaculate Conception is not explicitly stated in the Gospel, the *actual fact* of it does exist there implicitly, and the two-fold work of Christian devotion and theological speculation tends to bring it forth. In reading the Gospel a question comes to mind: can God-made man, who is Incarnate Purity, take his flesh from a body stained by sin? Now Mary, so far as we can judge, is a model of all virtue. From the very beginning of the Church both pious souls and learned writers recognized this, and is not the idea of the Immaculate Conception implicit in the very nature of her role in the divine plan,

[2] Is there need to state that this declaration is not concerned, in any sense, with the Virgin Birth of Christ of which we read in the Gospel? The two concepts are frequently confused.

in the manifestation of her unparalleled holiness? So may be read, for example, these lines of Saint Augustine: "I wish, for the love of Christ, that the question of the Holy Virgin Mary having ever committed sin be not even raised. We know that a greater grace was given her in the conquering of sin in the fact that she was worthy to conceive and to bring forth Him who, most certainly, knew no sin whatsoever." It is more than likely that when he wrote these words the great bishop of Hippo had no more in mind than Mary's exemption from all personal fault, from all actual sin. Nevertheless, it is evident that his declaration anticipates the dogma of the Immaculate Conception, of which it may be called almost a prophecy, carrying with it foreknowledge of what was to come.

How did the strivings of generations of Christians manage to convey the concept of Mary's sinlessness from the implicit to the explicit realm? At the beginning, the dogma of original sin, to the understanding of which Augustine himself had made a large contribution, seemed to offer an insurmountable barrier. How could this dogma (which underlies that of the universality of the Redemption) be reconciled with the declaration of so amazing an exception? Was Mary, a daughter of Eve, a woman of flesh and blood, outside the current of the redeeming flood? Yet if, on the other hand, she too was encompassed within its salvific action, must it not be because she had been born under the law of Sin? So convincing did this reasoning seem that some great scholars—and among them several devout clients of Mary—rejected the notion of the Immaculate Conception. Such were Saint Bernard, the mystic who so loved Mary, and his follower, Saint Bonaventure; such were Saint Albert the Great and Saint Thomas Aquinas. But the notion of the birth of the Most Pure Jesus having been marked by the sign of sin proved vexatious to the devout conscience. Valiant efforts were made to find an acceptable formula and it was suggested that Mary, although conceived in subjection to the state of original sin,[3] was nonetheless sanctified and free from every stain of evil from the time her soul and body were conjoined, being yet within the womb of her mother; but such subtle attempts proved unsatisfactory to minds and hearts alike. It was the theologian Duns Scotus who, in the thirteenth century, being spurred and sustained by the lively movement of devotion to Our Lady which characterized the Franciscan Order to which he belonged, actually championed the concept of Mary's Immaculate Conception. He showed how all the logical objections which had been voiced against this doctrine could be overcome; and he demonstrated the way in which this privilege of Our Lady flowed, for reasons of congruity or seemliness, from the very role which she plays in the Gospel.

Afterwards, this concept continued to develop within the ambit of the Christian consciousness, and it took on all the characteristics of a certitude. In the sixteenth century, the Council of Trent indicated, when it asserted the universality of original sin as being one of the indubitable concepts of Christian faith, that the terms of its decree on the subject were not intended to apply to the case of the Holy Virgin. The mystical writers of the French school of the seventeenth century, like Cardinal de Bérulle, Corneille in his verses on *Ève et Marie,* and Bossuet, when preaching before the Sorbonne, as well as a great many others, testified that they

---

[3] [That is to say, apparently, in the state of the mere absence of the supernatural gifts which God had showered upon Adam prior to his fall from grace and not in subjection to the *positive* consequences of that fall, particularly concupiscence or the proneness to sin characteristic of the generality of mankind since Adam.—A.G.]

believed in the Immaculate Conception. By the nineteenth century, this thesis had sent its roots so deeply into the Christian soul that a long process of clarification had been effected, and the words of Pope Pius IX seemed to almost all the faithful as no more than the expression of what they themselves already believed. In this way, and as a consequence of repeated efforts on the part of men, truth revealed itself under the guidance of Faith's mysterious leading. And this is, in general, the usual process by which Tradition perfects knowledge.

Another example, equally meaningful, is at hand in the development of belief in the Assumption of the Virgin Mary.

It is well-known that on Wednesday, November 1, 1950, Pius XII, in the presence of an immense throng gathered in Saint Peter's Square in Rome, and speaking in the exercise of his Infallible Office, defined and proclaimed the dogma of the Assumption of the Blessed Virgin Mary. He specifically declared it to be a truth of faith—and these terms are more than once repeated in the text of his Constitution, *Munificentissimus Deus*—that "the Immaculate and ever-virgin Mother of God, when she had come to the end of her earthly pilgrimage, was raised in soul and in body to heavenly glory." We may well ponder upon the words *in soul and in body* in order to establish them in their proper historical and doctrinal framework.

Before All Saints' Day of 1950, the Assumption of the Holy Virgin was, as need not be said, known and celebrated in all parts of the Catholic world. But what was understood by it? It appears clear enough that this belief covered a positive fact which concerns the earthly end of Christ's Mother. What did this mean? And how had Christians become aware of it even though it is not reported by Holy Scripture? By consulting the official declarations of the Church as they are to be read in the liturgical formularies appointed for the feast celebrated on August 15, it becomes apparent that the statement of it is direct and guarded. *Assumpta est Maria in coelum*, "Mary has been raised up to heaven," are the words of the Alleluiatic Verse and the Offertory of the Mass; and the antiphon for the Magnificat at Vespers is a repetition, in equally restrained terms, of this idea. Yet it is quite certain that in the minds of the majority of Catholics much more than this was implied. Père Jugie, who is one of the leading specialists on this question, sums up "the incomprehensible certitude of the Assumption in its essential nature" by declaring: "Mary, the Mother of God, conceived immaculately, is living glorified in her body and soul in heaven, following her departure from this earth." It may be noted that these terms are without prejudice in respect to both the exact time of the Assumption and the manner in which her leaving earth was actually effected.

How did this concept win to itself the consent of the Christian consciousness? There are three elements to be considered. According to Père Neubert,[4] "Some theologians have posited a local tradition about the Assumption, going back to the age of the Apostles and, little by little, spreading throughout the Church. They see in this the only way to explain the universal adherence to this truth. The existence of such a tradition is by no means to be discounted even though no trace of it be found in the older church writers. These writers did not make any mention of either the death or the burial of the Virgin. Now these are events which could not have passed unnoticed in the society in which Mary's final days on earth were passed. The thought of the Holy Virgin was

[4] P. E. Neubert: *Marie dans le dogme* (Paris, 1945); nouv. ed., p. 285.

very closely linked to the remembrance of the well-beloved Master; and it was too generally felt that all generations were to call her blessed to make it at all likely that her death would excite no attention from those around her, or that they would be lacking in interest in the burial of the body which had formed the body of Christ. It is by no means beyond belief that Saint John and perhaps some of the other Apostles, as well, may have been present when Mary died and that they had subsequently been given some revelation of the state of glory into which her body had entered. It is a very natural thing, also, that general curiosity would concern itself with the place of Mary's burial and that this would lead men to look into her tomb. Now there is an old tradition in Jerusalem which purports to reveal the precise place of Mary's burial and asserts her tomb to have been found empty, just as was that of the glorified Saviour.

"Nevertheless," continues Père Neubert, "these are no more than hypotheses, and they are not necessarily linked to belief in the Assumption of Mary."

If, however, according to the learned remarks we have just read, the traditions which concern the Assumption are hypothetical, what other species of development can be relied upon as justifying knowledge of the fact before the proclamation of the dogma? A whole complexus of concepts, psychological, scriptural, and theological, can have led to the unveiling of this idea. The devotion of Christian hearts, interpreting the feelings of Our Lord by analogy with their own, find in the love which our Saviour had for his Mother an argument to be read in the light of what we may call the heart's reason. The mere reading of Scriptural texts, when carefully done, inclines one in the same direction: the glorification of Mary by her Assumption is quite in line with the other privileges which were given her, and it seems to be the seal and the crown of her unexampled virtues. It was, therefore, only to be expected that through research into Scripture and the facing of its deep-seated concepts, theological speculation would become thoroughly acquainted with this.

In its essential nature, the theological fact of the Assumption of Our Lady is linked to two capital doctrines of the Christian faith: Mary's divine Maternity, and the resurrection of the body. Pius XII was careful to state very clearly these two "dogmatic kernels"; and it is not to be denied that the peculiar propriety of the recent definition being proclaimed in our day rests especially in its affirmation that the flesh of man will rise from the grave and will fulfill its destiny in a state of spiritual glory, this definition being expressed in opposition to the many doctrinaire attempts nowadays to limit man's bodily activities exclusively to those which are sordidly earth-bound. But although these two dogmas seem, in some sense, to presuppose that of the Assumption, it is nonetheless quite true that from the standpoint of history itself, it was not all at once that the exactions of this presupposition made themselves felt among men.

During the three first centuries we find nothing of any importance which concerns the Assumption. It is only as one studies certain Patristic passages that one is on the way to uncovering what Père Cayré has called "the embryonic stage" of belief in the Assumption. Even as late as the fifth century there does not seem to have been observed in the Church any feast of the Assumption or of the "Falling Asleep of Our Lady." The death of Our Lady was conceived of as having taken place in the most natural and simplest way, even though some seem to have thought that she might have died as a martyr.[5] However, toward the end of the fourth century, a priest in Jerusalem called Timothy asserted that "the Virgin is to this day living immortally"; and Saint Epiphanius, moreover, who was also a Palestinian, a native, that is to say, of a land where such traditions might well exist, wrote thus enigmatically of this subject: "Scripture tells us nothing of Mary's death because the exalted nature of that wonder causes the human mind to bow in stupefaction." [6]

It was in the sixth century, during the notable increase in devotion to Mary which followed the Council of Ephesus, that the Assumption became known throughout the Church as a concept more and more widely accepted. At this time, according to available evidence, the devotion of the faithful began to concern itself with this theme and to surround it with veneration. Spurred by the impulsion of this fervent

[5] This was due to taking in a baldly literal sense the prophecy of Simeon: "And thine own soul a sword shall pierce" (Luke II; 35).

[6] Reference should here be made to the scholarly study which Père Cayré offered to the Canadian Marian Congress (1948) and published in l'Année théologique under the title "L'Assumption aux quatre premiers siècles: état embroyennaire de la doctrine." After having considered successively the announcement of Mary in Genesis (III; 15-16), the paragraphs which Saint Luke devotes to her, Saint Paul's Epistle to the Romans (VIII), and the Apocalypse, then passing to a study of the relative silence of the first three centuries, the references made by the early Fathers and finally the insight reported by Saint Epiphanius and the assertion of the priest Timothy, Père Cayré reaches this conclusion: "As a matter of fact, Holy Scripture is not entirely silent: it speaks, however, in a manner which is wholly implicit. During the first centuries the doctrine of the Assumption remained in an embryonic state and underwent development of which the first traces are observable only in the fourth century. This development took place under conditions which guarantee on the one hand continuity and on the other preservation of purity of source; for *contrary to what is ordinarily said, legend plays no part here.* Although, as it appears, characteristics of this kind do not, of themselves, suffice as convincing evidence of the revealed nature of a doctrine, they can at least serve as a foundation quite sufficient to afford the Church an opportunity to speak with authority in this sense." In pointing out that this thesis has been contested by some, he finishes his remarks by saying: "We will leave to the Church the task of being herself the judge in such a case."

feeling, embodying the result of theological speculation, and basing themselves perhaps on some existing traditions while mingling with them certain data drawn from popular fancy, the apocryphal writers began to put into circulation the texts concerned with the *Passing of Mary.* The liturgy also now takes notice of this notion. Was this under the influence of the Apocrypha? There are those who think so, among them Père Jugie who writes: "The early feast of the Dormition of Our Lady seems to have indeed been introduced at the leading of these apocryphal accounts of the *Passing of Mary.* The Church made use of these more or less trustworthy narratives in order to propagate increased veneration for the Virgin and to augment the number of festivals in her honor." Very ancient liturgical books of the Gallic Church, dating from the seventh century, find place for a feast of the Assumption, and at Rome, from the reign of Saint Gregory (590-604), that feast would seem to have been observed on August 15. Thinkers, mystics, and theologians joined in testifying to this mystery. So many are they that it is not possible to mention them all. Saint Germanus, Patriarch of Constantinople, Saint Andrew of Crete, Saint Theodore the Studite, are among those who first began to write beautifully of the Assumption. This current of devotion, despite its obscure origin and modest beginnings, was destined henceforth to swell and gradually to course widely throughout all Christianity.

What was the situation before the proclamation of the Dogma in 1950? After more than a thousand years of thought, of comment, of explanation—whose history I shall not here attempt to retrace [7]—what elements were worth retaining for the knowledge they are able to convey? The Assumption of

[7] It may be found in the book by Père Jugie to which reference is made in the Bibliographical Note.

Our Lady clearly belonged among the great doctrinal ideas of Christianity as understood by Catholics and Orthodox Greeks. "For centuries," writes Canon Coppens, "the Church has quietly adhered to this doctrine." It had been definitively incorporated into the liturgy; the feast kept on August 15 is even regarded in some Christian lands as being one of the best loved of all. It is actually one of those on which, in some parts of France, men are seen to go to Mass who scarcely ever enter a church on other days. Some of the leading religious orders have dedicated their work to God under the patronage of Mary assumed into heaven; such is the case with the Augustinians of the Assumptions or Assumptionists.

Notwithstanding this, professed interpretation of the fact of the Assumption was far from being clear, and a good many divergencies could be discovered by comparing the opinions of the theologians. The opinion most commonly held was that which Père Neubert had summed up by saying: "In affirming the doctrine of the Assumption, we declare that the resurrection of the body for which we all look at the end of the world, took place, in Mary's case, very shortly after her death, just as with Jesus, save that Jesus arose and ascended into heaven by his own power while Mary did so by the power of her Son. From this fact arises the use of two different words: *ascension* and *assumption*. Therefore, like Jesus, the Holy Virgin enjoys from that time forward the reward which, at some as yet unknown period, will be the reward of all the just." In a broad sense this expresses the opinion of many theologians, among whom Le Hir may be named. Others, like Canon Coppens, are more restrained in their expression of the thesis, while Père Jugie, without saying so in so many words, hints by his use of the interrogative mode that the Holy Virgin may not have undergone death at all: "All that theology obliges us to affirm is that Mary possesses, as does her Son the Redeemer, a body passible and mortal, a body subject to suffering and death. Did she actually die? Theologically, the question remains unanswered."

On these different interpretations, no more than on the very essence of the doctrine, the Church had not yet taken a position by action of her infallible teaching authority. It is beyond doubt, however, that a strong tendency existed in favor of a dogmatic proclamation. The definition of this Marian privilege had been listed as one of the objectives of the Vatican Council; but as is well known, it remained one of the unfinished items on that Council's agenda. In his Encyclical on the Mystical Body of Christ, Pope Pius XII spoke of belief in the bodily assumption of Our Lady as being held universally when he exhorted: "Let us then beg the most Holy Mother of all Christians . . . who now lives resplendently in glory of body and soul with her Son in heaven, to increase her prayers to Him." And on May 1, 1946, the Pope wrote to all bishops throughout the world asking them to let him know, as speedily as possible, what would be their own feeling and that of their people concerning the definability of the Assumption and the propriety or opportuneness of proclaiming it as a dogma of faith. This request—recalling a request of the same sort which Pius IX had made before he proclaimed the dogma of the Immaculate Conception—was received enthusiastically by a large number of the prelates addressed. It appears that there existed, in this case, an open and undisputed expression of the common agreement of the Catholic consciousness which the Church has ever considered to be the living manifestation of Tradition.

And this is the chief argument employed by Pius XII in

justification of the definition: "Therefore, from the universal agreement of the ordinary teaching authority of the Church there is to be drawn a strong and definite argument in proof that the corporeal Assumption of the Blessed Virgin Mary into heaven is a truth revealed by God." Divine revelation is not wholly confined within the framework of the Scriptures. It extends itself and shows itself through the Church, the mystic bride of Christ, who is its constant vessel and abode. The leaven of more than a thousand years had done its work; and so it was that the Assumption of the Holy Virgin is now numbered among the precious truths of faith as a consequence of a development logically undeniable and based upon age-old tradition finally guaranteed by an authority which is infallible.[8]

[8] A more particularly theological aspect of devotion to Mary, currently under discussion, is pointed out by the learned Professor René Draguet of Louvain in his *Histoire du dogme catholique:* "Theology in our own day is faced with an analogous problem concerning the share of the Virgin in the actual work of the Redemption and in the distribution of its fruits. Account must be taken particularly of concepts traditionally held which have long regarded Mary's maternity as evidence for a kind of cooperation on her part, in both Incarnation and Redemption, which is moral as well as material. This tradition sees a parallel between Eve's role in the fall of man and Mary's role in his salvation. It, therefore, speaks of Mary as Co-Redemptrix and as Mediatrix of all graces. The Church has not yet definitively and authoritatively intervened in the discussion of these problems."

In a footnote Professor Draguet adds the remark: "There are some contemporary theologians who state the principle of Mary's participation in the work of human salvation very strongly: they make Mary a joint Principal, subordinated however to Christ, in the acquisition of redemptive merit. Discussion to which this theory has given rise (cf. W. Goossens: *De cooperatione immediata Matris Redemptoris ad redemptionem objectivam quæstionis controversae perpensatio* [Paris, 1939], indicates very well the hesitations and uncertainties as well as the venturesomeness of Christian speculation in its search for clarity and definition in the precise meaning of concepts which it seeks to formulate."

TWELVE

MARY AND OURSELVES

SUCH THEN ARE THE FINAL MATTERS which we must consider
in our effort to study Mary's personality within that glorious
half-light in which we see her. It is by no means certain,
however, that the discussion of these last concepts has really
fixed the attention of the devout, of those souls who, in the
veneration which they faithfully offer to the Holy Virgin,
are animated by considerations other than those which stem
from intellectual curiosity. As has been observed by Canon
Coppens, a wise professor of Dogmatic Theology: "Since the
epoch of the Counter-Reformation, Catholics in general have
been but little attracted by purely theological problems and
controversies; and on the whole this aloofness has worked
for good." From the historical point of view it is not the
apostolic and patristic origins of devotion to Mary, nor the
transcendent philosophical notions propounded about her
by the most learned of the doctors of theology which are of
greatest account: more significance is rather to be descried
in that overpowering current of fervor which has gathered
throughout the centuries and which we nowadays see rising

[114]

in unabated waves throughout the whole Catholic world.

And we must, moreover, take note of a fact of observation of compelling forcefulness. It has seemed to many that insofar as Western society is concerned, the nineteenth and twentieth centuries have been on the whole an era of religious decline, a time of ebbing faith; [1] nevertheless this has been, as well, a period in which devotion to Our Lady has increased very notably and has been manifested in numerous and diverse ways, a period in which this spirit of devotion has been expressed by those best qualified to voice it. It was at the very point of realization of the extent to which what Pius XI had called "the major scandal" of dechristianization had weaned away so many of the laboring class—and in great measure of the peasantry as well—that apparitions of Our Lady set off a spark which rekindled faith in thousands of hearts. First at the rue du Bac in Paris, and then successively at La Salette, Lourdes, Pontmain, and but yesterday at Fatima, the protecting figure of Mary the Holy Virgin hovered above prayerful throngs. All this was apparent to the historian as an irrefutable fact of existence. And it was also just at this time, as there opened in Europe that sinister epoch which Nietzsche, the prophet of extinction, had called "the Age of God's death," that Christian intellectuality poured itself forth most abundantly in praise of Mary. Masterpieces began to come from the hands of novelists like Huysmans, Léon Bloy, and Bernanos, of poets like Francis Thompson, Francis Jammes, and Paul Claudel, of scholars like Pierre Termier.

It cannot be claimed, of course, that all is of equal value in this outburst of fervent devotion. In literary matters alone

[1] It may be suggested, of course, that compensation for this is to be seen in the deeper and more cultivated knowledge of the modern believer.

one cannot dissent from the observation of the Abbé Brémond who writes: "Alas! how the mediocrities flourish! They have spoiled the finest subjects for us by their insipid twaddle, by their vulgarity, by their idle babbling." [2] Some of these wholesale manifestations, surrounded by a distastefully theatrical apparatus, have been the despair of many excellent Christians who have succumbed under their onslaught.

Notwithstanding this necessary reservation, the unusual proliferation of devotion to Mary in our own time is a fact of considerable and noteworthy significance. Any attempt to define its lines would have to begin with the observation that the primary role now appears to be taken neither by the data of dogmatic knowledge, nor by concepts purely theological. When he spoke of Mary and her Assumption, Bossuet was moved to cry out: "All the certitudes of Christian faith are linked together, and that which we now celebrate is particularly linked to the Incarnation of the Word." Believers certainly know and they freely admit that the figure of Mary as she is presented to them in all her perfections by the Church, is closely associated with all the great and mysterious truths of religion. But as they murmur an *Ave Maria* they are no longer dominated by merely speculative thought, and the outpouring of their love for the Virgin Mother Mary has an entirely different tone and meaning.

When Péguy, as a foot soldier, was marching along the road to Beauce repeating, in time with his marching, the lingering verses of *La Tapisserie,* the ideas which he expressed in words which are unforgettable were not those which speculative curiosity or confident learning summon up in the mind of the theologian. What welled up within him and pressed forward eagerly on his lips in an outrush that

[2] Henri Brémond: *L'École française,* p. 91.

would not be denied, was the determined will to find a manifestation of love and protection amidst the sorrows and
troubles of life. It was, as well, that deep-seated need which
the human spirit knows when, aghast at the ruinous work
of its own pride, it seeks to turn from evil, to abase itself,
to frame a plea for mercy. Beyond the wheat fields of Beauce,
Our Lady of Chartres gave to her pilgrim something which
sufficed for his solace.

When he was yet a boy, Père Léonce de Grandmaison,
destined to show himself in his lifetime so great a man in
God, began a lovely prayer to Our Lady with the words:
"Keep alive in me the heart of a child." And, in substance,
this is what is asked of Mary by all who turn to her as a
mediatrix, and who ask that she preserve in them that child-
like spirit which Christ promised to reward with the Kingdom of Heaven. She to whom they breathe this prayer in
humble confidence is, after we have penetrated beneath all
the trappings and sifted through all the commentaries, none
other than she whom we have met in the words of Saint Luke,
none other than the Virgin Mother, simple and worthy of
our confidence, shown to us in the Gospel.

So it is that finally all the attempts which might be made
to plumb the depths of Mary's character return to the original source, to that compelling image of the Virgin who by
her acquiescence in the demand made of her by the angel
became the spokesman for all mankind to whom God's promise had been addressed. These attempts find their answer in
her who is all love, in that young Mother whose solitary
selflessness guarded the Child against the dangers of the
world into which she ushered him. In those few pages of
Holy Writ the presence of Mary is really felt by the attentive
reader. They convey a total sense of her presence in all the

fullness of those characteristics which draw devout souls to her. And, as far as other things are concerned, those concepts and notions which study and thought strive to add to the data of Revelation, it is enough to repeat what has been said by one of the most penetrating thinkers and writers among the seventeenth century French mystics, Cardinal de Bérulle: "From the inmost depths of my soul I pay homage to you according to God's own ordinance, and in fitting acknowledgment of what your Greatness demands."

PART II

The Documents Which Tell of Mary

ONE

THE CANONICAL SCRIPTURES

The following pages contain the brief passages in the Canonical texts which speak of Mary. Their moving reticence is all the more striking if it be set side by side with the wordiness of the Apocrypha.

1. THE ANNUNCIATION

LUKE I; 26-38

After having told of the miraculous conception, by Zachary and Elizabeth, of John, the future Baptist, Saint Luke continues:

Now in the sixth month the angel Gabriel was sent from God to a town of Galilee called Nazareth, unto a virgin betrothed to a man named Joseph, of the house of David; and the virgin's name was Mary. And he went in unto her and said, 'Hail, full of grace, the Lord is with thee.' [1] And she

[1] The words "Blessed art thou amongst women" are not found in the best manuscripts, at this point; they derive from Elizabeth's greeting to Mary which the Evangelist reports later.

[121]

was troubled at his word and asked herself what manner of salutation this might be. And the angel said to her, 'Fear not, Mary, for thou hast found favour before God. And behold, thou shalt conceive in thy womb and shalt bring forth a son; and thou shalt call his name Jesus. He shall be great, and shall be called Son of the Most High; and the Lord God shall give to him the throne of David his father, and he shall reign over the house of Jacob for ever, and of his reign there shall be no end.' And Mary said unto the angel, 'How shall this be, seeing that I know not man?' And the angel answered and said to her, 'The Holy Spirit shall come upon thee, and the might of the Most High shall overshadow thee. Therefore the holy one to be begotten shall be called Son of God. And behold Elizabeth, thy kinswoman, she also hath conceived a son in her old age, and she who was called barren is in her sixth month; for "naught shall be impossible with God." ' And Mary said, 'Behold the handmaid of the Lord; be it done to me according to thy word!' And the angel departed from her.

2. THE VISITATION

LUKE I; 39-56

Now, in these days Mary arose and went with haste into the hill-country, to a town of Judah. And she entered the home of Zachary and saluted Elizabeth. And it came to pass that when Elizabeth heard the salutation of Mary, the babe in her womb leapt and Elizabeth was filled with the Holy Spirit, and she lifted up her voice with a loud cry and said, 'Blessed art thou among women, and blessed the fruit of thy womb! And whence this to me, that the Mother of my Lord should come unto me? For behold, when the sound of thy salutation fell on mine ears, the babe in my womb leapt with gladness. And blessed art thou who hast believed, for what the Lord hath promised thee shall be accomplished.'

And Mary said:

My soul doth magnify the Lord, and my spirit hath exulted in
    God my Saviour
Because he hath regarded the lowliness
    of his handmaid: yea, behold, henceforth
    all generations shall call me blessed:
Because he who is mighty hath wrought
    great things for me,
    and holy is his name:
And for generation upon generation is his mercy,
    unto them that fear him.
He hath put forth his arm powerfully:
    he hath scattered the proud in their heart's conceit:
He hath cast down monarchs from their thrones,
    and the lowly he hath exalted.
He hath filled the hungry with good things,
    and the rich he hath sent away empty.
He hath come to the aid of Israel, his servant,
    mindful of his mercy
(Even as he promised unto our fathers) to Abraham
    and to his seed for ever.

And Mary stayed with her about three months, and returned to her own home.

3. JOSEPH'S FEARS

MATTHEW I; 18-25

Now the coming of Jesus Christ was in this wise. When Mary his Mother was betrothed to Joseph, before they came together she was found with child from the Holy Spirit. And Joseph, her husband, being a just man and unwilling to expose her, purposed to put her away quietly. But whilst he was thus minded, behold, an angel of the Lord appeared to him in a dream, saying, 'Joseph, son of David, fear not to take unto thee Mary thy wife; for what has been begotten in her is from the Holy Spirit. She shall bring forth a son, and thou shalt call his name Jesus, for he shall save his people from their sins.' And all this came to pass that thereby might be fulfilled what was spoken by the Lord through the prophet, saying,

Behold the virgin shall conceive and bring forth a son, and they shall call his name Emmanuel, which translated is 'God with us.'

And Joseph arose from sleep and did as the angel of the Lord had commanded him and took unto him his wife. And he knew her not till she brought forth a son; and he called his name Jesus.

4. THE BIRTH OF JESUS

LUKE II; 1-7

Only those parts of Saint Luke's text in which Mary appears are given here.

Now it came to pass that in those days there went forth an edict from Caesar Augustus for the registration of the whole world. This first registration occurred when Quirinius was governor of Syria. So all went to enregister themselves, every man to his own town. And Joseph likewise went up from Galilee into Judæa, from the town of Nazareth to the town of David which is called Bethlehem—for he was of the house and family of David—to enregister himself together with Mary his betrothed, who was with child. And it came to pass that whilst they were there she completed the days of her delivery and brought forth her first-born son; and she swathed him round and laid him in a manger, because there was no place for them in the inn.

5. THE SHEPHERDS

LUKE II; 8-20

And in the same district were shepherds living out in the fields and keeping the night-watches over their flocks. And an angel of the Lord stood by them, and the glory of the Lord shone about them, and they feared with a great fear. And the angel said to them, 'Fear not, for behold, I bring you glad tidings of a great joy which shall be to all the people; for there hath been born to you this day a Saviour, who is Christ the Lord, in the town of David. And this shall be to you a sign thereof: ye shall find a babe enswathed and lying in a manger.' And suddenly there appeared with the angel a multitude of the heavenly host praising God and saying, 'Glory to God in the highest, and peace upon earth among men of his good pleasure!'

And it came to pass that when the angels had departed from them into heaven, the shepherds said one to another, 'Let us go, then, to Bethlehem and see this thing which is come to pass, which the Lord hath made known to us.' So they went with haste and found Mary and Joseph, and the babe lying in a manger. And when they had seen, they made known what had been told them concerning this child. And all that heard marvelled at what was told them by the shepherds. But Mary stored up all these things in her heart and pondered them. And the shepherds returned, glorifying and praising God for all that they had heard and had seen, even as had been told them.

6. THE PRESENTATION IN THE TEMPLE

LUKE II; 22-35

And when 'their days of purification had been completed' according to the Law of Moses, they brought him up to Jerusalem to present him to the Lord, as it is written in the Law of the Lord, 'Every male that openeth the womb shall be called holy to the Lord'; and to offer for sacrifice, according to what is said in the Law of the Lord, 'a pair of turtle-doves or two young pigeons.' And behold, there was in Jerusalem a man named Symeon, and this man was just and devout, awaiting the consolation of Israel, and the Holy Spirit was upon him, and it had been revealed to him that he should not see death before he had seen the Christ of the Lord. And he came in the Spirit to the temple; and when his parents brought in the child Jesus, to carry out the custom of the Law in his regard, himself also received him into his arms and blessed God and said:

> Now thou dost dismiss thy servant, O Master,
>   according to thy word, in peace;
> Because mine eyes have seen thy salvation,
>   which thou hast prepared before the face
>   of all the peoples:
> A light of revelation unto the gentiles,
>   and of glory for thy people Israel.

And his father and mother marvelled at the things that were said concerning him. And Symeon blessed them, and

[126]

he said unto Mary his Mother, 'Behold, this child is set for the fall and for the rise of many in Israel, and for a sign that shall be contradicted—yea, and thine own soul a sword shall pierce—that the thoughts of many hearts may be revealed.'

7. THE MAGI

MATTHEW II; 1-12

Now when Jesus was born in Bethlehem of Judaea in the days of King Herod, there came Magi from the East to Jerusalem, saying, 'Where is he that hath been born king of the Jews? For we have seen his star in the East and are come to worship him.' Upon hearing this, King Herod was troubled, and all Jerusalem with him. And he gathered together all the high priests and scribes of the people, and enquired of them where the Christ was to be born. And they said to him, 'In Bethlehem of Judaea; for so it is written through the prophet:

And thou Bethlehem, land of Judah, art no wise least among the rulers of Judah;
For from thee shall come forth a ruler, who shall tend my people, Israel.

Then Herod called the Magi secretly and learned from them the exact time when the star had appeared. And sending them to Bethlehem, he said, 'Go, and make careful enquiry concerning the child, and when ye have found him let me know, that I too may come and worship him.' So, after hearing the King they departed; and behold, the star which they had seen in the East moved on before them till it came to rest over the spot where was the child. And on seeing the

[127]

star they rejoiced with exceeding great joy. And entering the house, they saw the child with Mary his Mother, and falling down they worshipped him. And they opened their treasures and offered him gifts, gold and frankincense and myrrh. And being warned in a dream not to returned unto Herod, they withdrew to their own country by another way.

8. THE FLIGHT INTO EGYPT

MATTHEW II; 13-15; 19-20

And after their withdrawal, behold, an angel of the Lord appeared in a dream to Joseph, saying, 'Arise, take the child and his Mother, and flee into Egypt, and there remain until I tell thee; for Herod is about to seek the child in order to destroy him.' So he arose and took the child and his Mother by night and withdrew into Egypt, and there he remained until the death of Herod, that thereby might be fulfilled what was spoken by the Lord through the prophet, saying, 'Out of Egypt I called my son.'

And when Herod was dead, behold, an angel of the Lord appeareth in a dream to Joseph in Egypt, saying, 'Arise, take the child and his Mother, and go into the land of Israel; for they are dead that sought the life of the child.'

9. NAZARETH

MATTHEW II; 22-33

But Joseph hearing that Archelaus was King of Judaea in the place of his father Herod, he feared to go thither, and being warned in a dream, he withdrew into the district of Galilee. And he came and dwelt in the town called Nazareth.

The Annunciation, Attributed to Jan van Eyck, 1385-1441, Metropolitan Museum of Art, New York City.

Head of the Virgin, by Bernardino
Luini, 1475?-1533?.

The Visitation by Domenico Ghirlandaio, 1449-1494.

The Nativity by Bernardino Luini, 1475?-1533?.

Adoration of the Shepherds (Detail) by Giorgione, 1478-1510. National Gallery of Art, Kress Collection, Washington, D.C.

Adoration of the Magi (Altar Wings) by the Master of Darmstadt Passion.

The Flight into Egypt by Giotto, 1266-1336.

The Presentation in the Temple by Benjamin West, 1738-1820.

Christ Among the Doctors
by Carl Bloch, 1834-1890.

Miracle at Cana by Francois le
Fond, 1850?-1900?.

The Descent From the Cross by Rembrandt van Rijn, 1606-1669, National Gallery of Art, Mellon Collection, Washington, D.C.

Assumption of the Virgin by Bartoleme Murillo, 1618-1682.

10. THE BOYHOOD OF JESUS:
THE FINDING IN THE TEMPLE

LUKE II; 40-52

And the child grew and waxed strong, filled with wisdom, and the grace of God was upon him.

And his parents were wont to go every year to Jerusalem at the feast of the Passover. And when he was twelve years old, they went up according to the practice of the feast; and when they had fulfilled the days and were returning, the boy Jesus remained in Jerusalem, and his parents knew it not. Thinking that he was in the caravan, they came a day's journey, and sought for him among their kinsfolk and acquaintance, and since they found him not, they returned to Jerusalem in search of him. And it came to pass that after three days they found him in the temple, seated in the midst of the teachers, both listening to them and asking them questions. And all that heard him were amazed at his intelligence and his answers. And upon seeing him they were struck with wonder; and his Mother said unto him, 'My child, why hast thou done so to us? Behold, thy father and I seek thee sorrowing.' And he said to them, 'How is it that ye sought me? Knew ye not that I must needs be in my Father's house?' And they understood not the word which he spoke to them. And he went down with them and came to Nazareth, and was subject to them. And his Mother stored up all these things in her heart.

11. THE MARRIAGE AT CANA

JOHN II; 1-12

After the beginning of the public life of Our Lord there is but one passage in the Gospels in which we see Mary in the foreground. Saint John tells us:

And on the third day there was a marriage at Cana of Galilee, and the Mother of Jesus was there. Now Jesus and his disciples were also invited to the marriage. And the wine failing, the Mother of Jesus saith to him, 'They have no wine.' And Jesus saith to her, 'What have I to do with thee, O woman? My hour is not yet come.' His Mother saith to the servants, 'Whatsoever he shall say to you, do ye.' Now six stone water-jars were set there, after the Jews' manner of purification, each holding two or three firkins. Jesus saith to them, 'Fill the jars with water.' And they filled them to the brim. And he saith to them, 'Draw now, and take to the chief steward.' And they did so. And when the steward had tasted the water become wine—and he knew not whence it came, but the servants who had drawn the water knew—he calleth the bridegroom and saith to him, 'Every man setteth forth good wine first, and after they have drunk freely, then that which is poorer, but thou hast kept the good wine until now.' This beginning of his signs did Jesus at Cana of Galilee; and he manifested his glory, and his disciples believed in him.

After this he went down to Caparnaum, he and his Mother and his brethren and his disciples; and there they remained not many days.

12. TWO ALLUSIONS TO THE MOTHER OF JESUS

LUKE VIII; 1, 4, 19–XI; 27, 28
MARK III; 31-35

And it came to pass thereafter that he [Jesus] went through every town and village preaching the good tidings of the kingdom of God. (Saint Luke VIII; 1). Now . . . a great multitude was coming together, and men from every town were resorting unto him. (Saint Luke VIII; 4). Now there came unto him his Mother and his brethren; and they could not reach him because of the multitude. (Saint Luke VIII; 19) . . . and standing without they sent unto him to call him . . . and they say to him, 'Behold, thy Mother and thy brethren without are seeking thee.' And answering he saith to them, 'Who is my Mother, and who are my brethren?' And looking around upon them that sat round about him he saith, 'Behold my mother and my brethren! Whosoever doth the will of God, he is brother and sister and Mother to me.' (Saint Mark III; 31-35).

And it came to pass that as he was saying these things, a certain woman lifted up her voice from the crowd and said to him, 'Blessed is the womb that bore thee, and the breasts that thou didst suck!' But he said, 'Nay, rather, blessed are they that hear the word of God and keep it!' (Saint Luke XI; 27-28).

13. AT THE FOOT OF THE CROSS

JOHN XIX; 25-27

We do not see Mary again until the last moment, when Saint John pictures her for us, as she is present at her Son's death:

Now there stood by the cross of Jesus his Mother, and his Mother's sister, Mary of Clophas, and Mary Magdalene. When Jesus therefore saw his Mother and the disciple whom he loved standing by, he saith to his Mother, 'Woman, behold thy son.' Then he saith to the disciple, 'Behold thy Mother.' And from that hour the disciple took her to his own.

[131]

14. AFTER THE DEATH OF JESUS

ACTS I; 12-14

There is a simple but precious passage in the Acts of the Apostles *which clearly indicates Mary's place in the Christian fellowship, and it indicates that she was present at the Miracle of Pentecost. Saint Luke tells us that, after the Ascension:*

Then they the disciples returned unto Jerusalem from Mount Olivet, as it is called . . . And when they had entered, they mounted to the upper room wherein they were staying, namely Peter and John and James and Andrew, Philip and Thomas, Bartholomew and Matthew, James the son of Alphaeus and Simon the Zealot and Judas the brother of James. All these were persevering with one accord in prayer, together with the women and Mary, the Mother of Jesus, and with his brethren.

A little further on the book of the Acts (Acts II; 1-4) describes for us the miracle of the Coming of the Holy Spirit:

And when the day of Pentecost was come, they were all gathered together in one place. And suddenly there came a noise from heaven as of the rushing of a blast of wind, which filled the whole house where they were seated. And there appeared to them tongues, as though of fire, which parted and sat upon every one of them. And they were all filled with the Holy Spirit . . .

From this time forward the Church of Christ is fully ready to go forth to conquer the world. Mary is present at this final point in the institution of the Church. Is there no other link between her and the Church?

[132]

15. THE WOMAN OF THE APOCALYPSE

APOCALYPSE XII; 1-17

In order to answer this question we must re-read Chapter XII of the Apocalypse in which Saint John foretells the conflict between a mysterious woman and a fearful dragon, a conflict during which the woman brings into the world a male child. In the direct sense this text applies quite truly to the Church which brings forth issue in the sufferings of the mystical Christ. But in the symbolic sense the parallelism which refers it to Mary was perceived at an early date, and both Saint Augustine and Saint Epiphanius declare that there is a supernatural resemblance between Mary and the Church. From this point of view this wondrously suggestive text forms a part of Marian literature.

And a great sign was seen in heaven: a woman clothed with the sun, the moon under her feet, and upon her head a crown of twelve stars. She is with child, and crieth out in her travail, and is in anguish of delivery. And another sign was seen in heaven—behold a great red dragon, having seven heads and ten horns, and upon his head seven diadems; his tail draweth after it the third part of the stars of heaven, and it cast them to the earth. And the dragon stood before the woman who was about to bring forth, in order that when she should bring forth he might devour her child. And she brought forth a male child, who is destined to rule all the nations with a rod of iron; and her child was caught up to God and to his throne. And the woman fled into the wilderness, where she hath a place prepared by God wherein she is to be nourished during a thousand two hundred and sixty days.

And a battle took place in heaven, Michael and his angels

[133]

battling with the dragon. And the dragon and his angels battled, and they prevailed not, nor was their place found any more in heaven. And he was cast down, the great dragon, the ancient serpent, he who is called Devil and Satan, he who seduceth the whole world—he was cast down to the earth, and his angels were cast down with him.

And I heard a loud voice in heaven, saying: 'Now are come the salvation and the might and the kingdom of our God, and the power of his Christ; because the accuser of our brethren hath been cast down, he who accuseth them day and night before our God. And they have conquered him through the blood of the Lamb, and through the word of their witness, and they loved not their life in face of death. Wherefore be glad, O ye heavens, and ye that dwell therein! Woe to the earth and to the sea, because the devil hath gone down to you in great fury, knowing that he hath but little time!'

And when the dragon saw that he was cast down to the earth, he pursued the woman that had brought forth the male child. And there were given to the woman the two wings of the great eagle, in order that she might fly into the wilderness, to the place where she is to be nourished a time and times and half a time, away from the serpent. Then the serpent cast out of his mouth, after the woman, water like a river, that she might be swept away in its flood. But the earth came to the help of the woman; the earth opened its mouth, and swallowed the river which the dragon had cast out of his mouth. And the dragon was wroth at the woman, and departed to make war with the rest of her seed, with them that keep the commandments of God and bear witness to Jesus.

SUPPLEMENT: PATRISTIC TEXTS

Although they do not appertain to Holy Scripture it never-theless seems useful to cite here the following three texts which have to do with the end of Our Lady's life and with the connection between her and the Church which is sug-gested by the Apocalypse. In any case, these texts are cer-tainly expressive of what the Church regarded as true as early as the end of the fourth century.

1. SAINT EPIPHANIUS (315-403)

This writer expresses himself as follows on the question as to whether Our Lady—had she been then alive, which is quite possible—might have gone with Saint John on his journey into Asia:

And should it seem to any that we are mistaken, let them search the Scriptures for themselves. Therein they will find neither the death of Mary, nor mention of whether she is dead or is not dead; nor of whether or not she has been buried.

When Saint John went to Asia, it is nowhere said that he was accompanied on this journey by the Holy Virgin (whence the author is reminded of the earthly end of Mary and is

[135]

led to greater precision in his thought on this subject):

Holy Scripture is entirely silent on this point, because of the greatness of the wonder and in order not to disturb unduly the minds of men. As far as I am concerned, I dare not speak (of this wonder); I will keep my thoughts within me, and I will remain silent. It may be that we have even discovered enough about this holy and blessed woman to indicate that it is impossible to know if she be dead.

On the one hand, Simeon, as a matter of fact, said of her: "And thine own soul a sword shall pierce—that the thoughts of many hearts may be revealed" (Luke II; 35).

On the other hand, the Apocalypse of John declares that the dragon turned upon the woman who had brought the male child into the world, and that the wings of the eagle were granted unto the woman for inasmuch that she might flee into the desert so that the dragon could not lay hold upon her (Apoc. XII, 13 ff). It may be that this was accomplished in Mary. Nonetheless, I do not affirm it apodictically; and I will not declare that she lives immortally. Neither will I decide that she has died.

The Scripture, indeed, soars beyond the reach of the human mind and leaves this point in uncertainty, out of reverence for the incomparable Virgin, and to put an end to all unworthy and fleshly thought upon the subject.[1]

On the subject of Mary's earthly end, Epiphanius states:

"If the Holy Virgin had died and was buried, her falling asleep would have been surrounded with honor; death would

---

[1] Panarion (Haereses), 78, ch. xi; in Migne: p. 42; col. 715; [the present translation is by A.G. In his *La Mort et l'Assumption de la Ste. Vierge*, M. Jugie gives a French version of this and the passage cited below; but there is no available English translation.—A.G.]

have found her pure, and her crown would have been a virginal one.

"Had she been martyred according to what is written: 'Thine own soul a sword shall pierce,' then would she shine gloriously among the martyrs, and her holy body would have been declared blessed; for by her, in truth, did light come to the world.

"Or it might be that she is still alive; for to God nothing is impossible, and he is able to do whatever he wills. As a matter of fact, there is no one who knows the end of Mary." [2]

2. SAINT AUGUSTINE (354-430)

This great Doctor of the Church expresses himself as follows on the question of the comparison which is to be seen between Mary and the Church:

". . . may Christ help us, the Son of a Virgin, and the Spouse of virgins, born after the flesh of a virgin womb, and wedded after the Spirit in virgin marriage. Whereas, therefore, the whole Church itself is a virgin espoused unto one Husband Christ, as the Apostle saith (II Cor. 11; 2), of how great honor are its members worthy, who guard this even in the flesh itself, which the whole Church guards in the faith? which imitates the Mother of her Husband and her Lord. For the Church also is both a mother and a virgin. For whose virgin purity consult we for, if she is not a virgin? or whose children address we, if she is not a mother? Mary bare the Head of This Body after the flesh, the Church bears the members of that body after the Spirit. In both virginity

---

[2] Panarion (Haereses) 78, ch. xxiv; in Migne: p. 42; col. 737; [translation by A. G.]

hinders not fruitfulness; in both fruitfulness takes not away virginity. Wherefore, whereas the whole Church is holy both in body and spirit, and yet the whole is not virgin in body but in spirit; how much more holy is it in these members, wherein it is virgin both in body and spirit?" [3]

[3] [Augustine: *De Virginitate*, II, 2. The English translation is that of the Rev. C. L. Cornish, M.A. of Exeter College, Oxford, as given in *A Library of Fathers of the Holy Catholic Church, anterior to the division of the East and West; translated by members of the English Church* (Oxford: John Henry Parker, 1847); vol. 8; p. 309.—A.G.]

TWO

APOCRYPHAL TEXTS

Herewith are some of the chief apocryphal texts which have to do with Our Lady, and about which something has been said in Part I.

It should perhaps be pointed out again that none of these texts is to be taken at its face value; and this is true even of those which, like the Books of the Passing of Mary *contain nothing repugnant to faith. The reservations which have been insisted upon earlier ought not be lost sight of when there is a question of evaluating these texts.*

It is even well to emphasize the fact that the function of apocryphal literature is, from the doctrinal point of view, quite secondary; the thought of the Church Fathers, to whom is due the first essays in the development of dogma, is based solidly on the inspired text of canonical Holy Writ, and it is only occasionally that they make use of the Apocrypha. The development of dogma is not the outcome or a by-product of the folk-loric popular imagination: it is born of the utmost effort of the Christian intellect, enlightened by the Holy Spirit and basing itself solidly upon the data of Tradition, the while it ever strives to wrest, more and more thoroughly, the fullest meaning from the sacred text.

Nevertheless, the Apocrypha offer curious insights into the psychology of the Christian masses between the second and the seventh century, during which these writings came into being. It may be, moreover, that they have preserved fragments of age-old traditions; and it is beyond dispute that they have exercised a tremendous influence upon art, especially during the Middle Ages. At the present time, they are almost entirely unknown to the generality of readers.

1. THE BIRTH OF MARY, GLORIOUS MOTHER OF JESUS CHRIST, ACCORDING TO THE BOOK OF JAMES, OR PROTEVANGELIUM [1]

I. 1 In the histories of the twelve tribes of Israel *it is written that* there was *one* Ioacim, exceeding rich: and he offered his gifts twofold, saying: That which is of my superfluity shall be for the whole people, and that which is for my forgiveness shall be for the Lord, for a propitiation unto me.

2 Now the great day of the Lord drew nigh and the children of Israel offered their gifts. And Reuben stood over against him saying: It is not lawful for thee to offer they gifts first, forasmuch as thou hast gotten no seed in Israel. 3 And Ioacim was sore grieved, and went unto *the record of* the twelve tribes of the people, saying: I will look upon *the record of* the twelve tribes of Israel, whether I only have not gotten seed in Israel. And he searched, and found *concerning* all the righteous that they had raised up seed in Israel. And he remembered the patriarch Abraham, how in the last days

[1] M. R. James: *The Apocryphal New Testament.* (© Oxford: Clarendon Press, 1924); 38-49.

God gave him a son, even Isaac. 4 And Ioacim was sore grieved, and showed not himself to his wife, but betook himself into the wilderness, and pitched his tent there, and fasted forty days and forty nights, saying within himself: I will not go down either for meat or for drink until the Lord my God visit me, and my prayer shall be unto me meat and drink.

II. 1 Now his wife Anna lamented with two lamentations, and wewailed herself with two bewailings, saying: I will bewail my widowhood, and I will bewail my childlessness.

2 And the great day of the Lord drew nigh, and Judith her handmaid said *unto her:* How long humblest thou thy soul? The great day of the Lord hath come, and it is not lawful for thee to mourn: but take this headband, which the mistress of *my* work gave me, and it is not lawful for me to put it on, forasmuch as I am an handmaid, and it hath a mark of royalty. And Anna said: Get thee from me. Lo! I have done nothing (*or* I will not do so) and the Lord hath greatly humbled me: peradventure one gave it to thee in subtilty, and thou art come to make me partaker in thy sin. And Judith said: How shall I curse thee, seeing the Lord hath shut up thy womb, to give thee no fruit in Israel?

3 And Anna was sore grieved [and mourned with a great mourning because she was reproached by all the tribes of Israel. And coming to herself she said: What shall I do? I will pray with weeping unto the Lord my God that he visit me]. And she put off her mourning garments and cleansed (*or* adorned) her head and put on her bridal garments: and about the ninth hour she went down into the garden to walk there. And she saw a laurel-tree and sat down underneath it and besought the Lord saying: O God of our fathers, bless me, and hearken unto my prayer, as thou didst bless the womb of Sarah, and gavest her a son, even Isaac.

[141]

III. 1 And looking up to the heaven she espied a nest of sparrows in the laurel-tree, and made a lamentation with herself, saying: Woe unto me, who begat me? And what womb brought me forth, for I am become a curse before the children of Israel, and I am reproached, and they have mocked me forth out of the temple of the Lord? 2 Woe unto me, unto what am I likened? I am not likened unto the fowls of the heaven, for even the fowls of the heaven are fruitful before thee, O Lord. Woe unto me, unto what am I likened? I am not likened unto the beasts of the earth, for even the beasts of the earth are fruitful before thee, O Lord. Woe unto me, unto what am I likened? I am not likened unto these waters, for even these waters are fruitful before thee, O Lord. 3 Woe unto me, unto what am I likened? I am not likened unto this earth, for even this earth bringeth forth her fruits in due season and blesseth thee, O Lord.

IV. 1 And behold an angel of the Lord appeared, saying unto her: Anna, Anna, the Lord hath hearkened unto thy prayer, and thou shalt conceive and bear, and thy seed shall be spoken of in the whole world. And Anna said: As the Lord my God liveth, if I bring forth either male or female, I will bring it for a gift unto the Lord my God, and it shall be ministering unto him all the days of its life.

2 And behold there came two messengers saying unto her: Behold Ioacim thy husband cometh with his flocks: for an angel of the Lord came down unto him saying: Ioacim, Ioacim, the Lord God hath hearkened unto thy prayer. Get thee down hence, for behold thy wife Anna shall conceive. 3 And Ioacim gat him down and called his herdsmen saying: Bring me hither ten lambs without blemish and without spot, and they shall be for the Lord my God; and bring me twelve tender calves, and they shall be for the priests and for the

assembly of the elders; and an hundred kids for the whole people.

4 And behold Ioacim came with his flocks, and Anna stood at the gate and saw Ioacim coming, and ran and hung upon his neck, saying: Now know I that the Lord God hath greatly blessed me: for behold the widow is no more a widow, and she that was childless shall conceive. And Ioacim rested the first day in his house.

V. 1 And on the morrow he offered his gifts, saying in himself: If the Lord God be reconciled unto me, the plate *that is upon the forehead* of the priest will make it manifest unto me. And Ioacim offered his gifts and looked earnestly upon the plate of the priest when he went up unto the altar of the Lord, and he saw no sin in himself. And Ioacim said: Now know I that the Lord is become propitious unto me and hath forgiven all my sins. And he went down from the temple of the Lord justified, and went unto his house.

2 And her months were fulfilled, and in the ninth month Anna brought forth. And she said unto the midwife: What have I brought forth? And she said: A female. And Anna said: My soul is magnified this day, and she laid herself down. And when the days were fulfilled, Anna purified herself and gave suck to the child and called her name Mary.

VI. 1 And day by day the child waxed strong, and when she was six months old her mother stood her upon the ground to try if she would stand; and she walked seven steps and returned unto her bosom. And she caught her up, saying: As the Lord my God liveth, thou shalt walk no more upon this ground, until I bring thee into the temple of the Lord. And she made a sanctuary in her bedchamber and suffered nothing common or unclean to pass through it. And she called for the daughters of the Hebrews that were undefiled, and they carried her hither and thither.

2 And the first year of the child was *fulfilled,* and Ioacim made a great feast and bade the priests and the scribes and the assembly of the elders and the whole people of Israel. And Ioacim brought the child to the priests, and they blessed her, saying: O God of our fathers, bless this child and give her a name renowned for ever among all generations. And all the people said: So be it, so be it. Amen. And he brought her to the high priests, and they blessed her, saying: O God of the high places, look upon this child, and bless her with the last blessing which hath no successor.

3 And her mother caught her up into the sanctuary of her bedchamber and gave her suck.

And Anna made a song unto the Lord God, saying:

I will sing an hymn unto the Lord my God, because he hath visited me and taken away from me the reproach of mine enemies, and the Lord hath given me a fruit of his righteousness, single *and* manifold before him. Who shall declare unto the sons of Reuben that Anna giveth suck? Hearken, hearken, ye twelve tribes of Israel, that Anna giveth suck. And she laid the child to rest in the bedchamber of her sanctuary, and went forth and ministered unto them. And when the feast was ended, they gat them down rejoicing, and glorifying the God of Israel.

VII. 1 And unto the child her months were added: and the child became two years old. And Ioacim said: Let us bring her up to the temple of the Lord that we may pay the promise which we promised; lest the Lord require it of us (*lit.* send unto us), and our gift become unacceptable. And Anna said: Let us wait until the third year, that the child may not long after her father or mother. And Ioacim said: Let us wait.

2 And the child became three years old, and Ioacim said:
Call for the daughters of the Hebrews that are undefiled, and
let them take every one a lamp, and let them be burning, that
the child turn not backward and her heart be taken captive
away from the temple of the Lord. And they did so until they
were gone up into the temple of the Lord.

And the priest received her and kissed her and blessed her
and said: The Lord hath magnified thy name among all generations: in thee in the latter days shall the Lord make manifest his redemption unto the children of Israel. And he made
her to sit upon the third step of the altar. And the Lord put
grace upon her and she danced with her feet and all the house
of Israel loved her.

VIII. 1 And her parents gat them down marvelling, and
praising the Lord God because the child was not turned away
backward.

And Mary was in the temple of the Lord as a dove that is
nurtured: and she received food from the hand of an angel.

2 And when she was twelve years old, there was a council
of the priests, saying: Behold Mary is become twelve years old
in the temple of the Lord. What then shall we do with her?
lest she pollute the sanctuary of the Lord. And they said unto
the high priest: Thou standest over the altar of the Lord.
Enter in and pray concerning her: And whatsoever the Lord
shall reveal to thee, that let us do.

3 And the high priest took the vestment with the twelve
bells and went in unto the Holy of Holies and prayed concerning her. And lo, an angel of the Lord appeared saying
unto him: Zacharias, Zacharias, go forth and assemble them
that are widowers of the people, and let them bring every
man a rod, and to whomsoever the Lord shall show a sign,
his wife shall she be. And the heralds went forth over all the

country round about Judaea, and the trumpet of the Lord sounded, and all men ran thereto.

IX. 1 And Joseph cast down his adze and ran to meet them, and when they were gathered together they went to the high priest and took their rods *with them.* And he took the rods of them all and went into the temple and prayed. And when he had finished the prayer he took the rods and went forth and gave them back to them: and there was no sign upon them. But Joseph received the last rod: and lo, a dove came forth of the rod and flew upon the head of Joseph. And the priest said unto Joseph: Unto thee hath it fallen to take the virgin of the Lord and keep her for thyself. 2 And Joseph refused, saying: I have sons, and I am an old man, but she is a girl: lest I became a laughing-stock to the children of Israel. And the priest said unto Joseph: Fear the Lord thy God, and remember what things God did unto Dathan and Abiram and Korah, how the earth clave and they were swallowed up because of their gainsaying. And now fear thou, Joseph, lest it be so in thine house. And Joseph was afraid, and took her to keep her for himself. And Joseph said unto Mary: Lo, I have received thee out of the temple of the Lord: and now do I leave thee in my house, and I go away to build my buildings and I will come *again* unto thee. The Lord shall watch over thee.

X. 1 Now there was a council of the priests, and they said: Let us make a veil for the temple of the Lord. And the priest said: Call unto me pure virgins of the tribe of David. And the officers departed and sought and found seven virgins. And the priests called to mind the child Mary, that she was of the tribe of David and was undefiled before God: and the officers went and fetched her. And they brought them into the temple of the Lord, and the priest said: Cast me lots, which *of you* shall weave the gold and the undefiled (the white) and the fine linen and the silk and the hyacinthine, and the scarlet and the true purple. And the lot of the true purple and the scarlet fell unto Mary, and she took them and went unto her house.

[And at that season Zacharias became dumb, and Samuel was in his stead until the time when Zacharias spake *again*.]

But Mary took the scarlet and began to spin it.

XI. 1 And she took the pitcher and went forth to fill it with water: and lo a voice saying: Hail, thou that are highly favoured; the Lord is with thee: blessed art thou among women.

And she looked about her upon the right hand and upon the left, to see whence this voice should be: and being filled with trembling she went to her house and set down the pitcher, and took the purple and sat down upon her seat and drew out the thread.

2 And behold an angel of the Lord stood before her saying: Fear not, Mary, for thou hast found grace before the Lord of all things, and thou shalt conceive of his word. And she, when she heard it, questioned in herself, saying: Shall I *verily* conceive of the living God, and bring forth after the manner of all women? And the angel of the Lord said: Not so, Mary, for a power of the Lord shall overshadow thee: wherefore also that holy thing which shall be born of thee shall be called the Son of the Highest. And thou shalt call his name Jesus: for he shall save his people from their sins. And Mary said: Behold the handmaid of the Lord is before him: be it unto me according to thy word.

XII. 1 And she made the purple and the scarlet and brought them unto the priest. And the priest blessed her and said: Mary, the Lord God hath magnified thy name, and thou

[147]

shalt be blessed among all generations of the earth. 2 And Mary rejoiced and went away unto Elizabeth her kinswoman: and she knocked at the door. And Elizabeth when she heard it cast down the scarlet (*al.* the wool) and ran to the door and opened it, and when she saw Mary she blessed her and said: Whence is this to me that the mother of my Lord should come unto me? for behold that which is in me leaped and blessed thee. And Mary forgat the mysteries which Gabriel the archangel had told her, and she looked up unto the heaven and said: Who am I, Lord, that all the generations of the earth do bless me? 3 And she abode three months with Elizabeth, and day by day her womb grew: and Mary was afraid and departed unto her house and hid herself from the children of Israel. Now she was sixteen years old when these mysteries came to pass.

XIII. 1 Now it was the sixth month with her, and behold Joseph came from his building, and he entered into his house and found her great with child. And he smote his face, and cast himself down upon the ground on sackcloth and wept bitterly, saying: With what countenance shall I look unto the Lord my God? and what prayer shall I make concerning this maiden? for I received her out of the temple of the Lord my God a virgin, and have not kept her safe. Who is he that hath ensnared me? Who hath done this evil in mine house and hath defiled the virgin? Is not the story of Adam repeated in me? for as at the hour of his giving thanks the serpent came and found Eve alone and deceived her, so hath it befallen me also. 2 And Joseph arose from off the sackcloth and called Mary and said unto her O thou that wast cared for by God, why hast thou done this? thou hast forgotten the Lord thy God. Why hast thou humbled thy soul, thou that wast nourished up in the Holy of Holies and didst receive food at the hand of an angel? 3 But she wept bitterly, saying: I am pure and I know not a man. And Joseph said unto her: Whence then is that which is in thy womb? and she said: As the Lord my God liveth, I know not whence it is come unto me.

XIV. 1 And Joseph was sore afraid and ceased from *speaking unto* her (*or* left her alone), and pondered what he should do with her. And Joseph said: If I hide her sin, I shall be found fighting against the law of the Lord: and if I manifest her unto the children of Israel, I fear lest that which is in her be the seed of an angel, and I shall be found delivering up innocent blood to the judgment of death. What then shall I do? I will let her go from me privily. And the night came upon him. 2 And behold an angel of the Lord appeared unto him in a dream, saying: Fear not this child, for that which is in her is of the Holy Ghost, and she shall bear a son and thou shalt call his name Jesus, for he shall save his people from their sins. And Joseph arose from sleep and glorified the God of Israel which had shown this favour unto her: and he watched over her.

XV. 1 Now Annas the scribe came unto him and said to him: Wherefore didst thou not appear in our assembly? and Joseph said unto him: I was weary with the journey, and I rested the first day. And *Annas* turned him about and saw Mary great with child. 2 And he went hastily to the priest and said unto him: Joseph, to whom thou bearest witness [that he is righteous] hath sinned grievously. And the priest said: Wherein? And he said: The virgin whom he received out of the temple of the Lord, he hath defiled her, and married her by stealth (*lit.* stolen her marriage), and hath not declared it to the children of Israel. And the priest answered and said: Hath Joseph done this? And Annas the scribe said: Send officers, and thou shalt find the virgin great with child.

And the officers went and found as he had said, and they brought her together with Joseph unto the place of judgment. 3 And the priest said: Mary, wherefore hast thou done this, and wherefore hast thou humbled thy soul and forgotten the Lord thy God, thou that wast nurtured in the Holy of Holies and didst receive food at the hand of an angel and didst hear *the* hymns and didst dance before *the Lord,* wherefore hast thou done this?

But she wept bitterly, saying: As the Lord my God liveth I am pure before him and I know not a man. 4 And the priest said unto Joseph: Wherefore hast thou done this? And Joseph said: As the Lord my God liveth I am pure as concerning her. And the priest said: Bear no false witness but speak the truth: thou hast married her by stealth and hast not declared it unto the children of Israel, and hast not bowed thine head under the mighty hand that thy seed should be blessed. And Joseph held his peace.

XVI. 1 And the priest said: Restore the virgin whom thou didst receive out of the temple of the Lord. And Joseph was full of weeping. And the priest said: I will give you to drink of the water of the conviction of the Lord, and it will make manifest your sins before your eyes. 2 And the priest took thereof and made Joseph drink and sent him into the hill-country. And he returned whole. He made Mary also drink and sent her into the hill-country. And she returned whole. And all the people marvelled, because sin appeared not in them. 3 And the priest said: If the Lord God hath not made your sin manifest, neither do I condemn you. And he let them go. And Joseph took Mary and departed unto his house rejoicing, and glorifying the God of Israel.

XVII. 1 Now there went out a decree from Augustus the king that all that were in Bethlehem of Judæa should be recorded. And Joseph said: I will record my sons: but this child, what shall I do with her? how shall I record her? as my wife? *nay,* I am ashamed. Or as my daughter? but all the children of Israel know that she is not my daughter. This day of the Lord shall do as the Lord willeth. 2 And he saddled the she-ass, and set her upon it, and his son led it and Joseph followed after. And they drew near (unto Bethlehem) within three miles: and Joseph turned himself about and saw her of a sad countenance and said within himself: Peradventure that which is within her paineth her. And again Joseph turned himself about and saw her laughing, and said unto her: Mary, what aileth thee that I see thy face at one time laughing and at another time sad? And Mary said unto Joseph: It is because I behold two peoples with mine eyes, the one weeping and lamenting and the other rejoicing and exulting.

3 And they came to the midst of the way, and Mary said unto him: Take me down from the ass, for that which is within me presseth me, to come forth. And he took her down from the ass and said unto her: Whither shall I take thee to hide thy shame? for the place is desert.

XVIII. 1 And he found a cave there and brought her into it, and set his sons by her: and he went forth and sought for a midwife of the Hebrews in the country of Bethlehem.

2 Now I Joseph was walking, and I walked not. And I looked up to the air and saw the air in amazement. And I looked up unto the pole of the heaven and saw it standing still, and the fowls of the heaven without motion. And I looked upon the earth and saw a dish set, and workmen lying *by it,* and their hands were in the dish; and they that were chewing chewed not, and they that were lifting *the food* lifted it not, and they that put it to their mouth put it not

[151]

thereto, but the faces of all of them were looking upward. And behold there were sheep being driven, and they went not forward but stood still; and the shepherd lifted his hand to smite them with his staff, and his hand remained up. And I looked upon the stream of the river and saw the mouths of the kids upon *the water* and they drank not. And of a sudden all things moved onward in their course.

XIX. 1 And behold a woman coming down from the hill-country, and she said to me: Man, whither goest thou? And I said: I seek a midwife of the Hebrews. And she answered and said unto me: Art thou of Israel? And I said unto her: Yea. And she said: And who is she that bringeth forth in the cave? And I said: She that is betrothed unto me. And she said to me: Is she not thy wife? And I said to her: It is Mary that was nurtured up in the temple of the Lord: and I received her to wife by lot: and she is not my wife, but she hath conception by the Holy Ghost.

And the midwife said unto him: Is this the truth? And Joseph said unto her: Come hither and see. And the midwife went with him.

2 And they stood in the place of the cave: and behold a bright cloud overshadowing the cave. And the midwife said: My soul is magnified this day, because mine eyes have seen marvellous things: for salvation is born unto Israel. And immediately the cloud withdrew itself out of the cave, and a great light appeared in the cave so that our eyes could not endure it. And by little and little that light withdrew itself until the young child appeared: and it went and took the breast of its mother Mary.

And the midwife cried aloud and said: Great unto me to-day is this day, in that I have seen this new sight. 3 And the midwife went forth of the cave and Salome met her. And she said to her: Salome, Salome, a new sight have I to tell thee. A virgin hath brought forth, which her nature alloweth not. And Salome said: As the Lord my God liveth, if I make not trial and prove her nature I will not believe that a virgin hath brought forth.

XX. 1 And the midwife went in and said unto Mary: Order thyself, for *there is no small contention* arisen concerning thee.[2] And Salome made trial and cried out and said: Woe unto mine iniquity and mine unbelief, because I have tempted the living God, and lo, my hand falleth away from me in fire. And she bowed her knees unto the Lord, saying: O God of my fathers, remember that I am the seed of Abraham and Isaac and Jacob: make me not a public example unto the children of Israel, but restore me unto the poor, for thou knowest, Lord, that in thy name did I perform my cures, and did receive my hire of thee. 3 And lo, an angel of the Lord appeared, saying unto her: Salome, Salome, the Lord hath hearkened to thee: bring thine hand near unto the young child and take him up, and there shall be unto thee salvation and joy. 4 And Salome came near and took him up, saying: I will do him worship, for a great king is born unto Israel. And behold immediately Salome was healed: and she went forth of the cave justified. And lo, a voice saying: Salome, Salome, tell none of the marvels which thou hast seen, until the child enter into Jerusalem.

XXI. 1 And behold, Joseph made him ready to go forth into Judaea. And there came a great tumult in Bethlehem of Judaea; for there came wise men, saying: Where is he that

[2] (The italicized words are from the LXX Greek version of Isa. vii, which we render, 'Is it a small thing for you to weary men?' Immediately after is the prophecy, 'Behold, a virgin shall conceive,' &c., which accounts for the employment of the phrase here.)

is born king of the Jews? for we have seen his star in the east
and are come to worship him. 2 And when Herod heard it
he was troubled and sent officers unto the wise men. And he
sent for the high priests and examined them, saying: How is
it written concerning the Christ, where he is born? They say
unto him: In Bethlehem of Judaea: for so it is written. And
he let them go. And he examined the wise men, saying unto
them: What sign saw ye concerning the king that is born?
And the wise men said: We saw a very great star shining
among those stars and dimming them so that the stars appeared not: and thereby knew we that a king was born unto
Israel, and we came to worship him. And Herod said: Go
and seek for him, and if ye find him, tell me, that I also may
come and worship him. 3 And the wise men went forth. And
lo, the star which they saw in the east went before them until
they entered into the cave: and it stood over the head of the
cave. And the wise men saw the young child with Mary his
mother: and they brought out of their scrip gifts, gold and
frankincense and myrrh. 4 And being warned by the angel
that they should not enter into Judæa, they went into their
own country by another way.

XXII. 1 But when Herod perceived that he was mocked by
the wise men, he was wroth, and sent murderers, saying unto
them: Slay the children from two years old and under. 2 And
when Mary heard that the children were being slain, she was
afraid, and took the young child and wrapped him in swaddling clothes and laid him in an ox-manger.[3]

---

[3] From this point the *Protevangelium* is no longer concerned with Mary
but begins an account, in some brief chapters, of a certain Zachary of whom
Jesus had remarked (Matt. XXII; 35) that he was slain between the Temple
and the Altar. The apocryphal writers identified this Zachary with the
father of John the Baptist.

2. THE BOOK OF THE BIRTH OF BLESSED MARY AND OF THE CHILDHOOD OF CHRIST FROM THE GOSPEL OF PSEUDO-MATTHEW [1]

This work opens with a prologue attempting to establish that it was written by "the blessed Jerome, the priest" and that his purpose was to give a true account in contrast to the heretical teaching of certain "apocryphal books." However, according to many manuscripts, the prologue ends with the assertion that the author is "James, the son of Joseph." This contradicts what is said at the beginning; but it shows that the Latin version is entirely dependent upon the Protevangelium Jacobi, *and the only passages which will be given here either complete or modify what is already contained in the* Protevangelium.

In Chapter III, Joachim, while praying in the desert that the Lord will give him a son, receives word to return to Jerusalem. At the same time, Anne is warned that she is to go to meet her husband. Their "Meeting at the Golden Gate" is a frequent subject in medieval art. The chapter continues:

The angel which had already appeared to him while awake, appeared to him in sleep, saying, I am an angel and am given thee by God as a guardian; go down in confidence, and return to Anna, because the kind acts which thou and thy wife Anna have done are rehearsed in the presence of the Most High; and God will give you such fruit as neither the prophets nor any saint ever had from the beginning, nor shall have. Now when Joachim had awaked from sleep, he called all his herdsmen to him, and told them the dream. And they

[1] B. Harris Cowper: *The Apocryphal Gospels,* fifth edition (London: Frederic Norgate, 1881); pp. 34-64.

[155]

adored the Lord, and said to him, Take heed not to contemn the sayings of the angel any further. But arise, let us go hence, and let us return at a slow pace, feeding our flocks.

When they had tarried the space of thirty days on their return, and were now nigh,[2] behold, the angel of the Lord appeared to Anna as she stood and prayed, saying to her, Go to the gate which is called the Golden Gate,[3] and meet thy husband in the way, for today he will return to thee. She therefore went out in haste to meet him, with her maidens, and, praying to the Lord, she stood in the gate a long time waiting for him. When she was growing faint with very long expectation, she raised her eyes and saw Joachim afar off coming with his flocks; and she met him, and hung upon his neck, giving thanks to God, and saying, I was a widow, and lo, I am not one now; I was barren, and, behold, I have already conceived. So then, having worshipped the Lord, they entered the house. When this was heard, great joy was caused to all his neighbours and acquaintances, so that the whole land of Israel was gladdened by this report.

Chapter IV explains the seventh chapter of the Protevan-gelium, *where we are told that the child Mary did not cast a single backward glance when she went into the Temple:*

Now when nine months were completed after this, Anna brought forth a daughter, and called her Mary. When she had weaned her in her third year, Joachim and Anna his wife, went together to the temple of the Lord, to offer

---

[2] The thirty days of slow traveling here can hardly be reconciled with the five months mentioned in chap. ii.

[3] The Golden Gate is not regarded by modern writers as a gate of the city of Jerusalem, but of the temple. In the *Protevangelium,* chap. iv, the gate of Joachim's residence alone is intended, and in some copies distinctly affirmed.

sacrifices to God, and placed the babe that was named Mary in the apartment of virgins, wherein virgins continued day and night in the praises of God.⁴ When she had been set before the gates of the temple, she went up the fifteen steps ⁵ at such a rapid pace, that she did not at all look back, nor ask for her parents as is usual with infancy. Her parents, therefore, being anxious, and each of them asking for the infant, were both alike astonished, till they found her in the temple, so that even the very priests of the temple marvelled.

Chapter V is a thanksgiving canticle by Anne:

Then Anna was filled with the Holy Spirit in the sight of all, and said, The Lord Almighty God of hosts, being mindful of his word, hath visited his people with a good and holy visitation, to humble the hearts of the nations who rose up against us, and to convert them to himself. He hath opened his ears to our prayers, he hath banished from us the exultations of all our enemies. She that was barren is made a mother, and hath borne exultation and joy to Israel. Behold, I was set to offer gifts to my Lord, and my enemies could not prevent me. But God hath turned their heart towards me, and he hath given me eternal joy.

⁴ This tradition of young virgins being kept in the temple rests on no historical foundation, though it has been strongly defended by later writers.
⁵ The fifteen steps (quindecim gradus) correspond with the fifteen Psalms of *degrees* (Psalms 120-134). Some believe that there were fifteen steps leading from the court of women up to that of the priests. Other explanations have been offered, but no reliance can be placed upon the author, whom one reading makes to say, after mentioning the steps: "For there were about the temple—according to the fifteen Psalms of degrees—fifteen steps to ascend: the temple was on a mount, and there was constructed there the altar of burnt offering, which could not be reached from without except by steps." Comp. the Gosp. of the Nativity of Mary, chap. vi. This last statement about the steps around the altar is perhaps correct.

[157]

Chapter VI continues Mary's childhood:

Now Mary was in admiration with all the people of Israel.
When she was three years old, she walked with so firm a step,
spoke so perfectly, and was so assiduous in the praises of
God, that all were astonished at her, and marvelled; and she
was not regarded as a little child, but as an adult of about
thirty years, she was so earnest in prayer. And her face was
beautiful and splendid, to such a degree that scarcely any
one could look upon her countenance. Now she applied herself to wool-work, so that whatever the elder women could
not do, she accomplished when set to it in her tender age.
And she adopted this rule for herself, that she would continue in prayer from morning until the third hour; from the
third to the ninth she would occupy herself at her weaving
and from the ninth again she would apply herself to prayer.
Nor did she retire from prayer until an angel of God appeared to her, from whose hand she received food; and so
she advanced more and better in the work of God. Further,
when the elder virgins left off the praises of God, she did not
leave off, so that in God's praises and vigils no one was found
before her, nor any more skilled in the wisdom of God's law,
more humble in humility, more beautiful in singing, or more
perfect in all virtue. Indeed, she was constant, immoveable,
unalterable, and daily advanced to better things. None saw
her angry, or heard her reviling. For all her speech was so
full of grace, that God might be known to be in her tongue.
She was ever diligent in prayer and in searching of the law,
and was anxious not to sin by any word against her companions. Morever, she feared to make any mistake in laughter
or by the sound of her lovely voice, or lest any insult or pride
should show itself against her equals. She blessed the Lord

without intermission; and lest perchance even in her saluta-
tions she should cease from God's praise, if any one saluted
her, she answered by way of salutation, Thank God! From
her it first originated that men, when they would salute each
other, replied, Thank God! With the food which she daily
received from the hand of the angel she refreshed herself
alone; but she distributed to the poor the food which she
received from the priests. The angels of God were frequently
seen to talk with her, and they most diligently obeyed her.
If any one that was sick touched her, that same hour he returned home whole.

*In Chapter VIII Mary refuses a suitor and declares that
she has resolved to live in perpetual virginity.*

Now it came to pass, that when she was fourteen years of
age, and this gave occasion to the Pharisees to say that according to custom a woman of that age could not remain in
the temple of God, a decision of this kind was come to, that
a crier should be sent among all the tribes of Israel, (saying)
that all should meet on the third day, at the temple of the
Lord. Now when all the people had met, Abiathar, the high
priest, arose, and ascended to the upper step, so that he could
be heard and seen by all the people; and when great silence
was made, he said, Hear me, O children of Israel, and receive
my words in your ears. Since this temple was built by
Solomon, there have been therein virgins, the daughters of
kings, and the daughters of prophets, and of high priests, and
of priests, and they have been great and admirable. But when
they have come to a lawful age, they have been given in
marriage to husbands, and have followed the course of their
precursors, and have pleased God. But by Mary alone a new

order of life has been invented, and she promiseth God that she will remain a virgin. Wherefore it seems to me, that by our inquiry and the answer of God, we should seek to know to whom she ought to be committed to be kept. Then his saying pleased all the synagogue. And the lot was cast by the priests for the twelve tribes, and the lot fell upon the tribe of Judah. And the priests said, On the next day, let whoever is without a wife come and bring a rod in his hand. Wherefore it came to pass, that Joseph brought a rod along with the younger men. And when they had delivered their rods to the high priest, he offered sacrifice to the Lord God, and asked of the Lord; and the Lord said to him, Put the rods of all in God's holy of holies, and there let the rods remain, and bid them come to thee in the morning to receive their rods, and to him from the top of whose rod a dove shall come forth and fly to heaven, and in whose hand the rod, when returned, shall give this sign, Mary shall be delivered to be kept.

Now on the next day, when they all came early, and an offering of incense had been made, the high priest went into the holy of holies and brought out the rods. And when he had given a rod to each, and a dove had not gone forth from any, the chief priest arrayed himself with twelve bells and a priestly robe and went into the holy of holies and burned sacrifice and poured out prayer there. And an angel of God appeared, saying, There is here a very short rod which thou hast counted for nothing, and hast placed it with the rest, but hast not taken it out with the rest: when thou hast taken that out and given to him to whom it belongs, there shall appear in it the sign which I have spoken to thee of. It was the rod of Joseph, and because he was old he was as it were discarded, as though he could not receive it; but neither would he himself ask for his rod. And when he stood, humble and the last, the chief-priest with a loud voice cried to him, saying, Come Joseph, and receive thy rod, because thou art waited for. And Joseph came fearing, because the high priest called him with so very loud a voice. But straightway as he stretched out his hand to receive his rod, immediately a dove went forth from its top, whiter than snow and most beautiful, and fluttering a long time among the pinnacles of the temple, at last it flew towards the heavens. Then all the people congratulated the old man, saying, Thou art become blessed in thy old age, father Joseph, in that God hath shown thee fit to receive Mary. And when the priests had said to him, Take her, for out of all the tribe of Judah thou alone art elected by God, Joseph began to worship them with modesty, saying, I am old and have sons, and why do ye deliver to me this little child, whose age is less even than that of my grandchildren? Then Abiathar the chief priest said to him, Remember, Joseph, how Dathan and Abiram and Korah perished, because they contemned the will of God. So will it happen to thee if thou contemnest what is commanded thee by God. Joseph answered him, I do not contemn the will of God, indeed, but I will be her keeper until I know this by the will of God,—which of my sons can have her to wife. Let there be given her certain virgins of her companions for a solace, with whom she may meanwhile abide. Abiathar the chief priest answered, saying, Five [6] virgins shall be given, indeed, for her solace, until the day appointed cometh in which thou shalt take her, for she cannot be joined to another in matrimony.

Then Joseph took Mary with five other virgins, who were to be with her in the house of Joseph. Now these virgins were Rebecca, Zipporah, Susanna, Abigea, and Cael, to whom

[6] Seven virgins are assigned in the *Protevangelium*, chap. x.

there was given by the chief priest, silk and blue, and fine linen, and scarlet, and purple, and flax. And they cast lots among themselves what each virgin should do; and it fell out that Mary received the purple for the veil of the temple of the Lord. When she had received it, the virgins said, Since thou art the last, and humble, and less than all, thou hast deserved to receive and obtain the purple. And saying this, as though in a vexatious speech, they began to call her the queen of virgins. Therefore, while they did thus among themselves, an angel of the Lord appeared among them saying unto them, That saying shall not be uttered for vexing, but prophesied for a most true prophecy. Therefore, being terrified at the presence of the angel and at his words, they asked her to pardon them and pray for them.

The Protevangelium *is followed quite closely in Chapter IX, which tells of the Annunciation at the fountain; in Chapter X, which states that Joseph was a Capharnaum at "at work making tabernacles in the maritime regions; for he was a carpenter," although the* Protevangelium *states merely that he was employed in the timber yards. In the eleventh chapter we find the apparition of the angel to Saint Joseph, and it will be noted that the text shows a marked similarity to Saint Matthew I; 19 ff. Chapter twelve continues:*

After this there arose a great rumour that Mary was with child. And Joseph was laid hold of and led by the ministers of the temple, with Mary, to the chief priest, who together with the priests began to reproach him and to say, Why hast thou wronged her who is such and so eminent a virgin, whom as a dove the angels of God nourished in the temple, who would never see nor have a husband, and who had the best learning in the law of God? If thou hadst not done violence to her, she had still remained in her virginity. And Joseph took a solemn oath that he had never touched her at all. The chief priest Abiathar answered him, As God liveth, I will now cause thee to drink the water of the Lord's drinking,[7] and forthwith thy sin will appear.

Then there gathered together a multitude of people which could not be numbered, and Mary was brought to the temple. Now the priests, and her relatives and her parents, weeping said to Mary, Confess to the priests thy sin, thou who wast as a dove in the temple of God, and used to receive food from the hand of an angel.

Joseph again was called to the altar and there was given to him the water of the Lord's drinking, which when anybody who told a lie had tasted he went round the altar seven times, and God gave a certain sign in his face. When therefore Joseph had drunk it without fear, and had gone round the altar seven times, no sign of sin appeared in him. Then all the priests and attendants and people justified him, saying, Thou art become blessed, because no guilt is found in thee.

And they called Mary and said to her, And what excuse canst thou have? or what greater sign will appear in thee than this, that thy pregnancy betrayeth thee? This only we ask of thee, since Joseph is pure concerning thee, that thou shouldst confess who it is that deceived thee. For it is better that thy confession should expose thee, than that the anger of God should make thee manifest among the people by giving a sign in thy face. Then Mary confidently and intrepidly said, O Lord God, the King of all, who are conscious of secret things, if there is any pollution in me, or any sin, or any lust or immodesty, reveal me in the sight of all

[7] A Hebraism; for the water which the Lord commanded to be drunk.

peoples, that I may be an example for the correction of all. Having said this she approached the altar of the Lord with confidence, and drank the water for drinking, and went round the altar seven times, and there was found no spot in her.[8]

And when all the people were beside themselves with amazement, seeing her pregnancy and that no sign appeared in her face, the people began, with varied talk together, to be troubled. Some said she was holy and spotless, but others that she was bad and defiled. Then Mary, seeing she was held in suspicion of the people, and did not seem to them to be entirely cleared, said with a loud voice in the hearing of all, As the Lord Adonai liveth, the Lord of hosts in whose presence I stand, I have never known man; but I am known by Him to whom from my infancy I have devoted my mind. And I made this vow to my God from my infancy, that with him who created me I would abide in integrity, wherein I trust to live to him alone, and serve him alone: and as long as I live in him I shall abide without defilement. Then they all began to kiss her feet, and to embrace her knees, praying her to pardon their evil suspicions. And the people and priests and all the virgins led her with exultation and great joy to her house, crying out and saying, The name of the Lord be blessed for ever, for he hath manifested thy holiness to all his people Israel.

Chapter XIII tells of the order for the census, and of the journey to Bethlehem in a manner clearly based upon the Gospel according to Saint Luke. The detail of the grotto, borrowed from the Protevangelium, *is found here, as well as the offensive incident of the indiscreet midwife. This chapter*

[8] Lev. V; 14, etc.

ends with two paragraphs which are quite lovely: what we read of a bright star shining above the grotto recalls the custom of attaching a star to the Christmas Crib.

For the shepherds of sheep also declared that they had seen angels at midnight, singing a hymn, praising and blessing the God of heaven, and saying that the Saviour of all was born, which is Christ the Lord, by whom the salvation of Israel will be restored.[9]

Moreover, from evening until morning, a great star shone above the cave, and one so great had never been seen from the beginning of the world. And prophets who were in Jerusalem said that this star indicated the nativity of Christ, who should restore the promise, not only to Israel, but to all nations.

Chapter XIV is brief and supplies the curious detail of the ox and the ass:

Now on the third day after the nativity of our Lord Jesus Christ, the most blessed Mary went out of the cave, and, entering a stable, put her child in a manger,[10] and the ox and ass adored him. Then was fulfilled that which was spoken by Isaiah the prophet, who said, The ox doth know his owner, and the ass his master's crib.[11] The very animals, therefore, ox and ass, having him between them, incessantly adored him. Then was fulfilled that which was spoken by Habakkuk the prophet, who said, Between two animals thou art made known. In the same place Joseph tarried with Mary three days.

9 Luke II; 8, etc.
10 Luke II; 7.
11 Isaiah I; 3.

[165]

The two following chapters add little to Saint Luke's account. Chapter XV tells of the Presentation of the Child Jesus to the Temple. Simon is described as being two hundred years old and is said to have kissed the Child's feet. Chapter XVI describes the coming of the Magi just as do Saint Luke and the Protevangelium *with one addition: The divine Infant, in thanking them for their gifts, himself gives to each a little gold. Chapter XVII tells of the Massacre of the Innocents in language resembling that of Saint Matthew. But with the flight into Egypt (from Chapter XVIII through XXIV) there begins a series of marvelous additions to the Gospel:*

And when they had come to a certain cave and wished to rest in it, the blessed Mary came down from the beast, and sat and held the child Jesus in her lap. Now there were with Joseph three youths, and with Mary a certain damsel, who went on their way at the same time; and behold there suddenly came out of the cave many dragons, seeing which the youths cried out through excessive fear. Then Jesus, descending from his mother's lap, stood on his feet before the dragons, and they adored Jesus and then departed from them. Then was fulfilled that which was spoken by David the prophet, saying, Praise the Lord from the earth, ye dragons, ye dragons and all deeps.[12] And the little infant Jesus, walking before them, commanded them to hurt no man. But Mary and Joseph feared greatly lest perchance the little infant should be injured by the dragons. And Jesus said to them, Fear not, nor consider me because I am a little infant, for I was, and am ever perfect; it must needs be that all the wild beasts of the woods should grow tame before me.

[12] Ps. cxlviii; 7.

[166]

CHAPTER XIX

IN LIKE MANNER lions and leopards adored him, and kept
company with them in the desert; whithersoever Joseph and
blessed Mary went, they went before them, showing the way
and bowing their heads; and showing subjection by wagging
their tails, they adored him with great reverence. Now when
Mary saw lions and leopards and various kinds of wild beasts
coming round them, she was at first exceedingly afraid; and
Jesus with a glad countenance, looking into her face, said,
Fear not, mother; because they come not for thy hurt, but
they hasten to come for thy service and mine. By these sayings he removed fear from her heart. Now the lions walked
along with them, and with the oxen and asses, and the beasts
of burden which carried necessaries for them, and hurt no
one although they remained with them; but they were tame
among the sheep and rams which they had brought with them
from Judæa, and had with them. They walked among wolves
and feared nothing, and no one was hurt by another. Then
was fulfilled that which was spoken by the prophet: Wolves
shall feed with lambs; lion and ox shall eat chaff together.[13]
There were two oxen also with them, and a cart, wherein
they carried necessaries; and the lions directed them in their
way.

CHAPTER XX

NOW IT CAME TO PASS on the third day from their departure,
as they went along, the blessed Mary was wearied by the too
great heat of the sun in the desert; and seeing a palm tree
she said to Joseph, Let me rest a little under the shadow of
this tree. Joseph hastened therefore, and led her to the palm,

[13] Isa. xi; 6-9; lxv; 25.

and caused her to descend from the beast. And when the blessed Mary had sat down there, she looked at the foliage of the palm and saw it full of fruit, and she said to Joseph, I desire that I may be able to partake of the fruit of this palm. And Joseph saith to her, I wonder thou sayest this, when thou seest what a height the palm is, and that thou thinkest to eat of the fruit of the palm. I think more of scarcity of water, which is already failing us in the bottles, and we have not wherewith we may refresh ourselves and the beasts. Then the little child Jesus, sitting with a glad countenance in his mother's lap, saith to the palm, O tree, bend down thy branches, and with thy fruit refresh my mother. And straightway at this word, the palm bowed down its top to the feet of the blessed Mary, and they gathered from it fruit wherewith all were refreshed. Now after they had gathered all its fruit, it remained bowed down, waiting to rise at his command at whose command it had bowed down. Then Jesus said to it, Raise thee, O palm, and be strong, and be a partner with my trees which are in the paradise of my Father. And open from thy roots a spring of water which is hidden in the earth; and let waters flow forth from it to our satisfying. And immediately it arose, and there began to flow forth at its root a most pure fount of waters, very cool, and exceedingly clear. Now when they saw the fount of water they rejoiced with great joy; and they, and all the beasts and cattle were satisfied; wherefore they gave thanks to God.

CHAPTER XXI

ON THE NEXT DAY when they were departing thence, and at the hour wherein they began to pursue their journey, Jesus, turning to the palm tree, said, This privilege I grant thee, O palm, that one of thy branches should be taken by my angels, and planted in the paradise of my Father. And this

[168]

blessing I will confer upon thee, that unto all who have conquered in any contest, it may be said, Ye have attained the palm of victory.[14] As he said these things, behold, an angel of the Lord appeared, standing above the palm-tree; and taking away one of its branches, he flew to heaven having the branch in his hand. When they saw this they fell on their faces and became as dead. And Jesus spake unto them, saying, Why doth fear possess your hearts? Know ye not that this palm, which I have caused to be removed to paradise, will be prepared for all the saints in the place of delight, as it was prepared for us in this place of solitude? And they were filled with joy, and being strengthened, all arose.

CHAPTER XXII

AFTER THESE THINGS, as they pursued their journey, Joseph said to Jesus, Lord, this heat broils us: if it please thee, let us hold our course near the sea, that we may rest in the towns on the coast. Jesus said to him, Fear not, Joseph, I will shorten the way for you, so that what you were to go in the space of thirty days, you shall accomplish in this one day. While they said these things, behold, they looked forward, and began to see the Egyptian mountains and cities.

And they came, rejoicing and exulting, into the borders of Hermopolis,[15] and entered into a certain city of Egypt, which

[14] This account of the palm as a symbol of victory is of course an anachronism. Readers of Cicero, for example, will remember that he frequently employs the figure.

[15] There were in Egypt two or three cities with this name. The Church historian, Sozomen, who tells some of the stories current in his time, mentions the tree above referred to as having miraculous virtues; and he also mentions the story of the text. He says the tree was at Hermopolis in the Thebaid, near to which city its miraculous bowing down took place. He knows nothing of the marvelous journey reported in the first paragraph of this chapter. See Sozomen's Ecclesiastical History, book v, 20. Sotinen is in the text of Thilo the only name given, whence we may infer that it was regarded as the Egyptian name for Hermopolis. It is rather unfortunate for the story that the Thebaid was the upper province of Egypt.

is called Sotinen; and because there was no one known in it from whom they could have requested hospitality, they went into a temple, which was called the capitol of Egypt, in which temple three hundred and fifty-five [16] idols were placed, to which, on separate days, the honour of deity was rendered in sacrilegious rites. Now the Egyptians of that city entered the capitol, in which the priests admonished them how many sacrifices they should offer on each day according to the honour of their deity.

CHAPTER XXIII

Now it came to pass that when the most blessed Mary, with her little Infant, had entered the temple, all the idols were prostrate on the earth, so that they all lay upon their faces wholly shattered and broken, and so they showed evidently that they were nothing. Then was fulfilled what was spoken by the prophet Isaiah: Behold the Lord shall come upon a light cloud, and shall enter Egypt, and all the handiworks of the Egyptians shall be moved at his presence.[17]

CHAPTER XXIV

Then when it had been told to Aphrodosius the ruler of that city, he came with all his army to the temple. But when the priests of the temple saw that Aphrodosius, with all his army, came to the temple, they thought that he hastened only to see his revenge on those because of whom the gods had fallen. But he, having entered the temple, when he saw all the idols lie prostrate on their faces, drew nigh to the blessed

[16] Evidently a mistake for three hundred and sixty-five; one for every day in the year.
[17] Isa. xix; 1.

Mary, who bore the Lord in her lap, and adoring him, said to all his army, and to all his friends, If this were not the God of our gods, our gods would by no means have fallen on their faces before him, neither would they lie prostrate in his sight; wherefore, they silently avow him to be their Lord. We then, if we do not very carefully what we see our gods do, may incur the peril of his indignation, and may all come to destruction, as befel Pharaoh, king of the Egyptians; who, not believing such great miracles, was drowned with all his army in the sea. Then all the people of that city believed in the Lord God through Jesus Christ.

The following chapters (from XXV to XLII) are concerned with the boyhood of Jesus and embody a succession of marvelous stories in which he is the central figure. Some of these stories are attractive, as when Jesus is said to have fashioned birds out of clay and to have brought them to life so that they might fly. Others are disagreeable, as when he is shown get-ting even with a child playmate by causing him to die. Mary is frequently mentioned in these fables, and almost always in connection with the weariness which is caused to herself and Joseph by the Boy's superhuman powers. When the little Jesus is sent to school, he already knows the alphabet before the master teaches it to him, and he reverses their roles. When Joseph wishes to teach him his trade as a cabinet-maker and carpenter, the boy already knows more than he does. These legendary tales, which were later to be exag-gerated by the Gospels of the Infancy, *represent very well the* deliramenta apocryphorum, *those "mad dreams of the apoc-rypha" of which Saint Jerome speaks. They are not part of the subject with which we are presently concerned.*

[171]

3. A PASSAGE FROM THE ASCENSION OF ISAIAH

The following is the account of the Nativity given by this curious apocryphon. We have already discussed its relation to the retable at Aix-en-Provence. It will be recalled that something has been said above about the doctrinal tendencies of this work, which seems to have been always suspected of being more or less heretical.

CHAPTER XI

1. AFTER THIS I SAW, and the angel who spoke with me, who conducted me, said unto me: 'Understand, Isaiah son of Amoz; for for this purpose have I been sent from God.'[1] 2. And I indeed saw a woman of the family of David the prophet, named Mary, a Virgin, and she was espoused to a man named Joseph, a carpenter, and he also was of the seed and family of the righteous David of Bethlehem Judah. 3. And he came into his lot. And when she was espoused, she was found with child, and Joseph the carpenter was desirous to put her away. 4. But the angel of the Spirit appeared in this world, and after that Joseph did not put her away, but kept Mary and did not reveal this matter to any one. 5. And he did not approach Mary, but kept her as a holy virgin, though with child. 6. And he did not live with her for two months. 7. And after two months of days while Joseph was in his house, and Mary his wife, but both alone, 8. It came to pass that when they were alone that Mary straightway looked with her eyes and saw a small babe, and she was astonied. 9. And after she had been astonied, her womb was found as formerly before she had conceived.

[1] R. H. Charles: *The Ascension of Isaiah* (London: A. & C. Black, 1900); pp. 74-77.

10. And when her husband Joseph said unto her: 'What has astonied thee?' his eyes were opened and he saw the infant and praised God, because into his portion God had come. 11. And a voice came to them: 'Tell this vision to no one.' 12. And the story regarding the infant was noised abroad in Bethlehem. 13. Some said: 'The Virgin Mary hath borne a child, before she was married two months.' 14. And many said: 'She has not borne a child, nor has a midwife gone up (to her), nor have we heard the cries of (labour) pains.' And they were all blinded respecting Him and they all knew regarding Him, though they knew not whence He was. 15. And they took Him, and went to Nazareth in Galilee.

4. INFANCY GOSPELS[1]

From among the many "Infancy Gospels" (which are, for the most part, no more than versions and extensions of old apocryphal gospels, modified by successive editors) I have chosen some brief passages as illustrations or examples of Arabian, Syrian, and Armenian sources.

THE ANNUNCIATION

According to the Armenian text, the Virgin Mary held a lengthy discussion with the Angel before agreeing to receive the Holy Spirit. The chapter ends:

The angel said: 'O blessed and holy Virgin, hear these words, and keep within your heart what I have to say to you:

[1] Some of these passages appear in the standard English translations of the Apocrypha; of others it appears that there is no available English version. As is indicated in each case, the passages cited by M. Daniel-Rops are here presented in the version of B. Harris Cowper: *The Apocryphal Gospels* (London: Norgate, 1881), or in a translation made for the present work by A. G.

This is not the work of man, and what I shall tell you of is something that comes from no man. It is the Lord who will bring it to pass within you. He, himself, possesses power to withdraw you from all the sorrows of this trial.' Mary said: 'If the thing be as you say, and if it be that the Lord himself deigns to bow down toward his servant and his slave, then may it be done unto me according to your word.' And the angel left her.

At the very time that the holy Virgin so spoke and bowed herself in all humility, the Word of God entered within her through her ear, and the very nature of her body was sanctified, all her senses being purified as gold is tried in the fire. She became a temple of holiness, without stain, and the resting place of the divine Word. At this time the Virgin became heavy with child. The angel brought these good tidings to Mary on the 15 Nisan which would be the sixth of April,[2] on a Wednesday, at the third hour of the day.

There follows Our Lady's prayer:

"Now, after the holy Virgin had received tidings from the angel, she arose, and then, casting herself face downwards on the ground, she said: "O Lord of my soul and my body, yours is the power to do all things according to your will and your creative love. Freely do you govern all things according to your good pleasure. Deign, therefore, to bow presently to the

---

[2] Like the two dates, the synchronization is arbitrary. It may be that the Armenian editor has awkwardly modified the passage in order to make it agree with the calendar of his Church (the Annunciation being celebrated according to the Armenians on April 6, and Christmas on January 6). As far as the phrase "the Word of God entered within her through her ear" is concerned, it may be noted that it represents a strained attempt to represent the fact of the Conception of Jesus by Mary. From this may derive certain works of art like the Annunciation of Aix.

prayers of your slave: hear me and deliver my soul, because it is you who are the God of my salvation, and it is your name, O Lord, that I do daily call upon. To this time have I kept myself in holiness, in justice, and in purity, being resolved to preserve my virginity completely and wholly, for your sake, O Lord my God, and without any desire or wish of carnal defilement. And, now, may your will be done."

EVE AND MARY

In reporting this incident, the Armenian Book of the Infancy *was inspired by the concept that Mary is the "new Eve" destined to redeem the fault of the first Eve. This is a theme beloved of the early Fathers.*

How Eve, the mother of mankind, and Joseph came in haste to see the most blessed and holy Virgin Mary in her Motherhood.

Now when Joseph and the mother of our race saw this thing, they fell upon their faces, and they loudly thanked God, glorifying him and saying: "Blessed are you, O Lord God of our fathers, God of Israel; for, this day, by your coming you have redeemed man. You have restored me anew and lifted me up and re-established me in my original state. Now does my soul feel itself strong, and I thrill with hope in God my Saviour."

After she had spoken, Eve, the mother of the race, beheld a cloud rising above the grotto toward the heavens. And from the other side, there came forth a shining light which fixed itself above the manger. And the Child sought his Mother's breast, and drank her milk; and afterwards he went back to his place and stayed there. When they saw this, Joseph and Eve gave glory and thanks to God; and they wondered greatly

[175]

at the marvels which had come to pass. And they said: "Has anyone ever heard that such things can be, or has anyone ever seen what has now come about?"

And the mother of mankind entered into the cave and took the Child in her arms. And she began to caress and to embrace him with all gentleness. She gave thanks to God; for the Child was wondrous fair to see, his features being resplendent with the glory of his soul. Then she wrapped him again in the swaddling clothes and laid him again in the manger. And Eve, the mother of the race, went forth from the grotto. All at once she saw a woman called Salome who had come from the city of Jerusalem. And Mother Eve went up to her and she said: "I give you gladsome tidings: a young virgin, one who has never known man, has brought a child into the world, within this grotto."

There follows the scabrous episode of Salome, the midwife, similar to the account of it in the Protevangelium.

THE MAGI

Generally speaking, the episode of the Magi undergoes considerable development in the apocryphal literature of Syria, Armenia, and the Arabian lands. These were places which had contact with Persia whence had come these mysterious visitors. We, therefore, find certain details expressed in this text with precision: the Magi are Persian kings, they are three in number, and their names are known.

There is an old Arabic text in the Laurentian Library at Florence in which it is definitely stated that the Magi are of the religion of Iran and followers of the celebrated reformer, Zoroaster, who is made to predict the coming of the Messiah.

[176]

In the days of the prophet Moses, there lived a man named Zaradust (Zoroaster) who was the founder of an occult doctrine. On a certain day, as he was seated by the side of a fountain giving instruction to students of the occult, he interrupted his discourse to say to them: 'Behold a virgin shall conceive without having known man. She shall bring forth a child and, nevertheless, the seal of her virginity will remain unbroken; and these glad tidings shall be known in the seven regions of teh earth. The Jews will crucify this Child in the Holy City that was established by Melchisedech. He shall visit the regions of the dead and shall then ascend on high. As a sign that he has been born you shall see a star in the East, a star brighter than the sun and than all other lights which are in the sky, for as a matter of fact it will not be a star at all but rather an angel of the Lord. When you shall see it, then hasten toward Bethlehem. There you shall adore the newborn King and offer gifts unto him. The star will guide you to him.' Now these words foretold what was to occur, and Josuah the son of Nun declared that this Zaradust is none other than Balaam the astrologer. The prophecy was fulfilled in due time.

The Armenian version then gives in great detail the number and the names of the Magi, being in agreement here with some manuscripts of Pseudo-Matthew.

And an angel of the Lord went forth, with all haste, to the land of Persia in order to lead the Magian Kings who were on their way to adore the newborn Child. And they, being guided by the star for nine months, came to their journey's end just as the Virgin became a Mother. Now in those days, the Kingdom of Persia dominated all kings in Orient lands.

[177]

The Magian Kings were three brothers: the first Melkon,[3] who ruled over the Persians; the second, Balthasar, ruled the Indians; and the third, Gaspar, was lord of the Arabians. Being brought together by the command of God, they arrived at the moment the Virgin became a Mother. They had pressed forward on the journey and so they arrived exactly at the time Jesus was born.

The Armenian gospel continues with tiresome prolixity about the gifts of the Magi and their conversations with Mary and Joseph; but the Syriac manuscripts (of Mossoul in Mesopotamia and in the collection of the Royal Asiatic Society of London) supply further details about the Magi themselves. (The incident of the angel is briefly referred to in the Arabian gospel).

On that same night a guardian angel was sent into Persia. He showed himself to the people of that country under the appearance of a bright star which lit up all the land of Persia. Now on the 25th of the first kanoun—which is the day of Christ's birth—there was a great festival observed by the Persians in adoration of the sun and the stars. All the Magi, gorgeously attired, celebrated this solemnity in a magnificent manner. Suddenly, a great light shone out above them. They left behind the kings, the feasting and the rejoicing, and coming forth, they went out to see this great sight. They beheld a great and shining star which had risen on the land of Persia. Because of its brilliance it seemed like a great sun.

And in their own tongues the kings asked their priests: "What is this sign that we behold?" As if they were inspired they declared: "The King of Kings is born, the God of gods

[3] Of this name Westerners made Melchior.

is here, and the Light of lights has come. Behold how a heavenly being has come to us to tell us of his birth so that we may go to him and offer him our gifts and our adoration."

Thereupon chiefs, magistrates, and generals, all arose and said to the priests: "What presents ought we bring unto him?" And the priests replied: "Gold, and myrrh, and incense."

Three kings who were sons of the Persian kings, took up, as though mysteriously moved to do so, the first, three measures of myrrh, the second, three measures of gold, and the last, three measures of incense. They were apparelled in their most precious ornaments, they wore their crowns upon their heads, and in their hands they bore their gifts. At cock-crow they left their own country, accompanied by nine men, and they set out on their journey, being led by the star which had appeared to them. And in the strength of the Holy Spirit, the same angel who had removed the prophet Habakuk from Jerusalem and had brought food to the prophet Daniel languishing among the lions, led the Persian kings towards Jerusalem.

Having left Persia at the break of day, they entered into Jerusalem and they began to question the townspeople, saying: "Where is the newborn king whom we have come to see?" At these words all the people of Jerusalem became upset and were seized with fear. They therefore informed Herod the king, and he sent men to question the Persian kings and to bring them into his presence. He asked them, "Whence come you? Whom do you seek?"

They said: "We seek the king who is born in Judæa, in Jerusalem. One of the gods has told us of his birth so that we may come before this king to adore him and to give him our gifts." And Herod was affrighted at the tsight of the sons

[179]

of the Persian kings whom he saw crowned and bearing gifts in their hands as they sought a king born in Judæa. Herod and all his court were indeed alarmed at the sight of these sons of kings.

And Herod spoke unto them: "Great is the power of the king who has drawn you to come to offer homage to him. Verily he is a king and the king of kings. Go therefore and find him; and when you have done so, come to me so that I too may worship him."

However, Herod had resolved basely within his heart to slay the Child while he was yet young, and with him the Persian kings, as well; for he said within himself: "Then will I be lord of all the world."

The Magi left King Herod. And they saw the star which went before them until it stopped above the grotto. At this point, its form changed, and it became like a pillar of fire which reached from the earth even unto the heavens.

They entered within the grotto, and they found Mary, Joseph, and the Child who was wrapped in swaddling clothes and lying in a manger. They adored him and offered him their gifts; and they greeted Mary and Joseph. And Joseph and Mary were astonished to see the three sons of kings, wearing their crowns and kneeling in adoration before the new-born Child, even before they had enquired who he was. Joseph and Mary therefore said unto them: "Whence do you come?" And they answered, saying: "We are come from Persia." Joseph and Mary said: "When did you leave Persia?" The kings replied: "Yesterday evening we were celebrating a festival. After our feast one of the gods told us: 'Arise and go forth with gifts to the king who is born in Judæa.' The cock crew as we girded ourselves for the journey. We arrived in your presence just now, at the third hour of the day."

And Mary took one of the cloths in which Jesus was wrapped and she gave it them. From her hands they accepted it as a gift of great worth. And when the night of the fifth day of the week after the Nativity had come, the guardian angel who had shown himself in the form of a star returned to be their guide. They followed his leading in their return to their homeland, and they reached it at the time set for dining.

All Persia was glad of their return and was in great wonderment. Before sunrise all the kings and the priests gathered together and they said unto them: "How has it been with you on your journey and in your return? What have you done, and what is this that you bring back with you?" And then they showed them the swaddling cloth which Mary had given them. In the Magian manner they held high festival. They lit a great fire. Then they cast the cloth into the midst of the fire and they adored it as the cloth became like unto the fire. Then when the fire died out, they drew forth the cloth, whiter than snow and more firm even than it had been before. Having taken it up, they kissed it; and gazing upon it, they said: "Verily and without doubt, this is the garment of the God of gods inasmuch as the fire of the gods will not destroy it." And they preserved it in all faith and in deep reverence.[4]

ACCOUNT OF THE YOUNG MAN CHANGED INTO A MULE

This is the best known of the many "miraculous" events to which the mad imagination of the apocryphal authors gave birth. According to the Arabian gospel it is connected with the mediation of Our Lady. It affords a good example of all that is most doubtful in these stories as well as being illustrative of their vulgar popularity.

[4] Translation by A. G.

As they drew nigh to another city they saw three women coming, with weeping, out of a cemetery. On seeing them lady Mary said to the girl that accompanied them, Ask them what is their condition and what calamity has befallen them. And when they were asked by the girl they did not answer, but asked in turn, Whence are ye, and whither are ye going? for the day is now past, and night is coming on. We are travellers, said the girl, and seek a lodging wherein to pass the night. They said, Go with us, and lodge with us. They followed them therefore, and were led into a house which was new, and adorned and garnished with much furniture. Now it was wintertime, and the girl having entered the chamber of these women found them again weeping and lamenting. There stood by them a mule covered with a sumptuous cloth, sesame was placed before it, and they kissed it and gave it food. And the girl said O my ladies, What is the matter with this mule? They answered weeping and said, This mule which thou seest, was our brother, born of the same mother with us. For when our father died leaving us great wealth, we who had this only brother endeavoured to secure his marriage, and arranged a wedding for him after the manner of men. But the women, being moved with envy of one another, placed a charm upon him unknown to us, and one night, a little before daylight, when the doors of our house were shut, we saw that this our brother had been changed into a mule, such as thou now seest him. But we, in sorrow, as thou seest, having no father by whom we may be comforted, have left untried no learned magician or enchanter in the world, without sending for him; but it has profited us nothing. Now whenever our hearts are oppressed with grief, we rise and go with our mother, and after we have wept at the tomb of our father, we return.

When the girl had heard this, she said, Be of good cheer, and weep not: for a remedy for your trouble is at hand; yea, it is with you and within your house: for I also was a leper, but when I saw that woman and with her this little child whose name is Jesus, I poured upon my body the water with which my mother had washed him, and I was healed. Now I know that he can heal your affliction also. But arise, go to my lady Mary, and when she is brought into your house reveal your secret to her, suppliantly entreating her to have pity on you. And when the women heard what the girl said, they went in haste to my lady Mary, and brought her to them, and sat down before her weeping and saying, O our lady, lady Mary, have pity on thy servants, for there is no one older than ourselves, or head of the family surviving, nor is there father or brother to take care of us: but this mule which thou seest was our brother, whom the women by a charm have made what thou seest. We pray thee, therefore, have pity on us. Then lamenting their lot, lady Mary lifted up the Lord Jesus and put him on the back of the mule, and herself wept along with the women; and to Jesus Christ she said, Alas, my son, heal this mule by thy great power, and make him a man endued with reason as he was formerly. When these words proceeded from the mouth of my lady, lady Mary, the mule changed its form, and became a man, a young man, who was whole without any blemish. Then he and his mother and sisters adored my lady, lady Mary, and began to kiss the Child, holding him above their heads, saying, Blessed is thy mother, O Jesus, O Saviour of the world; blessed are the eyes which enjoy the happiness of beholding thee.

INCIDENT OF THE GOOD THIEF

Again the intervention of Mary is stressed in this episode by which this Arabic apocryphon attempts to offer an ex-

*planation of the different fates of the two thieves who were
crucified with Our Lord on Calvary.*

CHAPTER XXIII

HAVING DEPARTED THENCE, when they had come into a desert
country, and heard that it was haunted by robbers Joseph and
lady Mary thought to pass through this region by night. But
as they went, behold they saw two robbers lying in the way,
and with them a multitude of robbers who were their companions, asleep. Now the two robbers upon whom they came
were Titus and Dumachus. So Titus said to Dumachus, I
pray thee suffer these persons to depart freely, and so that
our companions observe them not. But when Dumachus refused, Titus said again, Take to thee from me forty drach-
mas, and hold this pledge. At the same time he held out to
him his girdle with which he was girded, that he should not
open his mouth nor speak. And when my lady, lady Mary,
saw that the robber showed kindness to them, she said to him,
The Lord God shall sustain thee with his right hand, and give
thee remission of sins. And the Lord Jesus answered and said
to his mother, After thirty years, O mother, the Jews will
crucify me at Jerusalem, and these two robbers will be lifted
on the cross with me, Titus at my right hand and Dumachus
at my left, and after that day Titus shall go before me into
Paradise.[5] And she said, God avert this from thee my son.

MANY MARIAN MIRACLES

*The "Infancy Gospels" recount numerous miracles accom-
plished at Mary's intercession. This one is taken from an
Arabian text. It is typical of its kind, and its conclusion indicates the manner in which the authors of the Apocrypha pre-*

[5] Luke xxiii; 39-43.

tended to explain every conceivable detail of the Canonical Scriptures.

Another woman there had two sons who fell sick, and one died but the other lived: so his mother took him up and, weeping, brought him to my lady, lady Mary, and said, O my lady, help and succour me. For I had two sons, one of whom I have now buried, but the other is nigh unto death. See how I will beg and pray to God. And she began to say, O Lord, thou art kind and merciful and good; thou gavest me two sons, but since thou hast taken one of them away, leave me at least this one. Therefore lady Mary, seeing the violence of her weeping pitied her, and said, Put thy son in my son's bed and cover him with his clothes. And when she had put him in the bed in which Christ was lying, and he was already dead and had closed his eyes, as soon as the smell of the garments of the Lord Jesus Christ reached the boy, he opened his eyes and, calling his mother with a loud voice, asked for bread, which he swallowed when he received it. Then said his mother, O lady Mary, now I know that the power of God dwelleth in thee, so that thy Son healeth men who are partakers of the same nature with himself, after they have touched his garments. This boy that was healed is he who in the Gospel is called Bartholomew.

THE BROKEN PITCHER

Some of these incidents are not wanting in charm: this tale may even be taken in a symbolic sense. It is thus reported in the Arabian text.[6]

[6] The translation of the four preceding passages is by B. Harris Cowper in his *The Apocryphal Gospels;* fifth edition (London: Frederic Norgate, 1881); pp. 186-189; 190; 195-196; 198.

My lady, Lady Mary, once commanded the Lord Jesus to go and fetch her some water from the well. But when he went to bring the water, his waterpot, which was already filled, was shattered and broken. But the Lord Jesus spread out his handkerchief, and took the water he had gathered up to his mother, who marvelled at the act. But she laid up and stored in her heart all that she saw.

MARY'S FEARS

The Arabian gospel ends rather suddenly, but the Armenian goes tirelessly on to embroider elements from the Protevangelium *and* Pseudo-Matthew *in reference to the flight into Egypt, the fall of the idols, and so forth. Then we are told of the return of the Holy Family to Palestine to the accompaniment of marvelous prodigies. We pass over these tales of the "miracles" of the Child Jesus, for Mary has no great role in them. She here appears to be distressed by them, and is depicted reproaching him.*

Mary said: "My son, you are but a child and have not yet come to man's estate. Do not act as though nothing matters, lest harm befall you." Jesus replied: "My Mother, your gloomy fears are unreasonable: I know all that will come about."

Mary said: "Be not grieved because of what I have said to you; I am so oppressed by forebodings of evil that I know not what to do." Jesus asked: "What plans do you have for me?" Mary answered: "It is because of this that I am disturbed: we have tried to teach you all manner of things during your childhood, and you have done nothing with our instructions. You have never applied yourself to anything. And now that you are growing older, what will you do? How will you manage to live?"

When he heard this Jesus became annoyed, and he said to his Mother: "Now you speak very thoughtlessly indeed. Do you not understand the signs and wonders I have done before you, which you have seen with your own eyes? And even so, you do not believe despite all the time I have been with you. You have seen my miracles; think of all that I have done and be patient yet awhile. You shall see the completion of all my work; but now, my time is not yet come. But as for you, continue to trust me." Having said this, Jesus went forth in haste from the house.[7]

5. HISTORY OF JOSEPH THE CARPENTER[1]

Many passages in this apocryphon, devoted to Saint Joseph, concern Our Lady; and they are particularly interesting as evoking a period which is almost entirely ignored by the canonical writers. There are many versions; but among them the best is perhaps an Arabic one which may have been based upon the Syriac. There is also a Coptic version which adds further details. The Arabic version is used here. It must be borne in mind that Jesus himself is supposed to be the speaker.

THE CHILD JESUS AT HOME WITH HIS PARENTS

CHAPTER XI

JUTUS AND SIMEON the elder sons of Joseph, having married wives, went away to their families. Both the daughters like-

---

[7] Translated by A. G.

[1] [The selections made by M. Daniel-Rops from this apocryphon are here presented in the English version of B. Harris Cowper: *Op. cit.;* pp. 107-8; 115; 116; 117-18. The translation of the *Summary of Saint Joseph's life* has been made by me for this book, and the same is true of the final passage in this section, the fregment concerning the "assumption" of Joseph.—A.G.]

wise married, and went to their houses. But Judas and James the Less, and the virgin my mother, remained in the house of Joseph. I also continued along with them, not otherwise than if I had been one of his sons. I passed all my time without fault. I called Mary my mother, and Joseph father, and in all they said I was obedient to them; nor did I ever resist them, but submitted to them, just as other men whom earth produceth are wont to do; nor did I provoke their anger any day, nor return any harsh word or answer to them; on the contrary, I cherished them with immense love, as the apple of my eye.

A SUMMARY OF SAINT JOSEPH'S LIFE

This is the exact sum of the days of the just man, Joseph. He lived for forty years unmarried. Before her death his wife lived with him for forty-nine years. One year after his wife's death, my Mother, the pure Mary, was confided to him by the priests that he might protect her until the time of her marriage. She dwelt in his house for two years. During the third year, while she was still with Joseph, that is to say in her fifteenth year, she brought me into the world in a fashion which no creature can understand; for it is known only to me, to my Father, and to the Holy Spirit, who dwell in me in unity.

The total number of years of my father, this just old man, were one hundred eleven, as was decreed by my heavenly Father. And it was on the twenty-sixth of the month of Abib that his soul left his body. *The fine gold began to lose its brightness, and the pure silver to tarnish;* it is of his intellect and his understanding that I speak. He turned away from food and from drink.

Mary is told that she too must die.

After the account of the death agony of Saint Joseph, the text goes on:

My mother, the unsullied virgin, rising and coming to me, said, O, my beloved son, this pious old man Joseph is already dying. And I replied, O, my mother, most loving, surely upon all creatures, which are born in this world, lieth the same necessity of dying: for death hath dominion over all the human race. Thou, also, O, my virgin mother, must expect the same end of life with all other mortals. Nevertheless, thy death, as also the death of this pious man, is not death, but perennial life for ever. But it behoveth me too to die, as respects the body which I received from thee. But arise, O, my venerable mother, go and enter to Joseph, the blessed old man, that thou mayest see what happeneth when his soul goeth up from his body.

The death of Joseph drew many sighs. And I held his hand for the space of one whole hour: and he, with his face turned towards me, signified that I should not leave him. Afterwards, placing my hand upon his breast, I perceived his soul already near his throat, preparing to depart from its receptacle.

Now when my virgin mother saw me touching his body, she also touched his feet; and finding them already half-dead, and without heat, she said to me, O, my beloved son, clearly his feet now begin to grow cold, and are like the coldness of snow. Then when his sons and daughters had been called, she said to them, Come, all of you, and approach your father: for certainly he is now come to his end. Assia, the daughter of Joseph, answered, saying, Woe, unto me, O, my brethren, surely this is the same disease as was that of my beloved mother. And she wailed and wept, and all the other children

[189]

of Joseph lamented with her. I also, and Mary my mother, wept with them.

JOSEPH DIES AND IS BORNE ALOFT BY THE ANGELS

And turning my eyes to the south side, I saw Death now coming, and all Gehenna with it, crowded with its host and attendants; and their garments, faces, and mouths cast out fire. When my father Joseph saw these come straight to him, his eyes were bathed in tears; and the same moment he groaned in a wonderful manner. Therefore, seeing the violence of his sighs, I repulsed Death, and all the host of followers which attended him. And I called upon my good Father, saying:

O Father of all mercy, Eye which seest, and Ear which hearest, hearken to my supplication and prayers for the old man Joseph; and send Michael, the prince of thy angels, and Gabriel, the herald of light, and all the light of thy angels; and let their whole order journey with the soul of my father Joseph, until they have brought it to thee. This is the hour wherein my father hath need of mercy. Now I say to you, that all saints, nay, all men that are born in the world, whether they be just or wicked, must needs taste death.

Therefore, Michael and Gabriel came to the soul of my father, Joseph; and, having received it, wrapped it in a bright wrapper. So he committed his spirit into the hands of my good Father, who bestowed upon him peace. And none of his children yet knew that he had fallen asleep. But the angels preserved his soul from the demons of darkness, which were in the way; and they praised God, until they brought it to the habitation of the pious.

A fragment from the Egyptian Sahidic version gives further details concerning the "assumption" of Joseph, clearly in imitation of that of Mary.

Therefore, after I had said *Amen,* which my dear Mother, Mary, repeated after me in the language of those who dwell aloft, all at once Michael and Gabriel came from heaven in the company of the angelic choir, and they ranged themselves about the body of my father, Joseph. Just then, constriction and depression pressed sorely upon him, and I knew that the final moment was come. He became a prey to pains like those which accompany labor. He was racked in agony as of a violent storm or of a great fire which consumes a forest of trees. Yet Death itself was not yet able to grasp the body of my dear father, Joseph, to separate it from his soul, because the Angel of Death on looking into the room beheld me seated at his head and stroking his forehead.

And I knew that the Angel of Death hesitated to come into my presence. Therefore, I crossed the threshold of the room, and I found Death waiting out there, alone and fearfully. I said to him: "You have come from afar; now enter quickly and do the will of my heavenly Father. But be as careful of Joseph as of your own eyes, for he is my father according to the flesh,[2] and ever since I was a child has he cared for me, even to the extent of fleeing with me from place to place to escape the murderous hand of Herod. And he has been my teacher, just as the fathers of other sons are their teachers, instructing them in the paths of righteousness." Then did

[2] This phrase indicates the untrustworthy character of this work, which may be influenced by even Arian ideas. In the canonical Gospels, Jesus is nowhere referred to as the son of Joseph "according to the flesh"; rather is it said that *he was taken to be his son* (Luke III; 23) or that *he was legally the son of Joseph* (Matt. I; 16).

Abbaton * enter in and he grasped the soul of my father, Joseph, sundering it peacefully from his body at the moment of sunrise, on the twelfth of the month of Ephiphi.

The whole of the days of life of my dear father Joseph are one hundred and ten years. Michael took the two corners of a cloth of fine silk, and Gabriel the other two corners, and they took the soul of my dear father Joseph and they wrapped it up in this cloth.

Of all those that were near him none knew that he was dead. Even Mary, my Mother, knew no more than the others. I ordered Michael and Gabriel to watch over the body of my dear father, Joseph, because there were brigands abroad; and I ordered heavenly spirits continually to sing about him until they should have borne him aloft to be with my heavenly Father.

6. THE BOOK OF THE PASSING OF THE MOST HOLY VIRGIN, THE MOTHER OF GOD [1]

Attributed to Saint Melito, bishop of Sardis in Lydia

Melito, servant of God, bishop of the church of Sardis, unto the brethren which are established in peace at Laodicea, reverend in the Lord, greeting.

I remember that I have oft-times written concerning a certain Leucius, who, after that with us he had been a companion of the apostles, with alienated sense and rash mind departed from the way of righteousness and put into his books many things concerning the acts of the apostles, and spake

---

* So is the Angel of the Abyss called (Apoc. IX; 11).

[1] The translation is that of the late Provost of King's and Eton; cf. M. R. James: *The Apocryphal New Testament* (Oxford: Clarendon Press, 1924); pp. 209-216.

many and diverse things of their mighty deeds, but concerning their teaching lied much, affirming that they taught otherwise, and establishing his own wicked position as if by their words. Nor did he account this sufficient, but also corrupted with so evil a pen the departure of the blessed Mary ever virgin, the mother of God, that it is unlawful not only to read but even to hear it in the church of God. We therefore at your petition have written simply those things which we heard from the apostle John, and have sent him unto your brotherhood: believing no alien doctrines which sprout out from heretics, but that the Father is in the Son, the Son in the Father, the triune person of godhead and undivided essence abiding: and that not two natures of man were created, a good and a bad, but that one good nature was created by a good God, which by the fraud of the serpent was corrupted through sin, and restored by the grace of Christ.[2]

II. When therefore the Lord and Saviour Jesus Christ for the life of the whole world hung on the tree of the cross pierced with nails, he saw standing beside the cross his mother and John the evangelist, whom he more especially loved beyond the other apostles because he alone of them was a virgin in body. Unto him therefore he committed the charge of the holy Mary, saying to him: Behold thy mother; and to her: Behold thy son. From that hour the holy mother of God continued in the especial care of John so long as she endured the sojourn of this life. And when the apostles had taken the world by their lots for preaching, she abode in the house of his parents beside the Mount of Olivet.

III. In the second year after Christ having overcome death had ascended into heaven, upon a certain day, Mary fervent

---

[2] The author here has in mind erroneous teaching about the Trinity propagated by the early heretics. He opposes also the doctrine of the Manicheans.

with desire of Christ betook herself alone into the refuge of her dwelling to weep. And lo, an angel shining in a garment of great brightness stood before her and came forth with words of greeting, saying: Hail thou blessed of the Lord, receive the greeting of him that granted salvation to Jacob by his prophets. Behold, said he, this palm-branch. I have brought it to thee from the paradise of the Lord, and thou shalt cause it to be carried before thy bier on the third day when thou shalt be taken up out of the body. For behold thy Son with the thrones and the angels and all the powers of heaven awaiteth thee. 2 Then Mary said to the angel: I ask that all the apostles of the Lord Jesus Christ be gathered together to me. And the angel said: Lo, this day by the power of my Lord Jesus Christ all the apostles shall come to thee. And Mary said to him: I ask that thou wouldest put thy blessing upon me, that no power of hell may meet me in that hour wherein my soul goeth out of the body, and that I may not see the prince of darkness. And the angel said: The power of hell shall not hurt thee; but an eternal blessing hath the Lord thy God given thee, of whom I am the servant and messenger: but think not that the power not to see the prince of darkness can be given by me, but by him whom thou didst bear in thy womb: for his is all power, world without end. And thus saying, the angel departed with great light. 3 Now the palm-branch shone with exceeding brightness. Then Mary put off her garments and clothed herself in her best raiment, and taking the palm which she had received of the angel's hand she went out into the Mount of Olivet and began to pray and to say: I was not worthy to receive thee, Lord, if thou hadst not had mercy on me; nevertheless I kept the treasure which thou didst commit to me. Therefore I pray thee, O king of glory, that no power of hell may hurt me. For

[194]

if the heavens and the angels quake before thee every day, how much more a man created of the earth, in whom is no good save what he hath received of thy bounty. Thou, Lord, art God, blessed for ever, world without end. And having thus said, she returned to her dwelling.

IV. And behold, suddenly, while Saint John was preaching at Ephesus, on the Lord's day, at the third hour, there was a great earthquake, and a cloud raised him up and took him out of the sight of all and brought him before the door of the house where Mary was. And he knocked at the door and straightway went in. But when Mary saw him she rejoiced greatly and said: I pray thee, my son John, remember the words of my Lord Jesus Christ wherewith he commended me to thee. For behold on the third day, [when] I am to depart out of the body—*and* I have heard the counsels of the Jews who say: Let us wait until the day when she shall die who bore that deceiver, and let us burn her body with fire. 2 So she called Saint John and took him into the secret part of the house and showed him her grave-clothes and that palm of light which she had received from the angel, and charged him to cause it to be borne before her when she should go to the tomb.

V. And Saint John said to her: How shall I alone prepare thy burial unless my brethren and fellow apostles of my Lord Jesus Christ come to pay honour to thy body?

And lo, suddenly by the commandment of God all the apostles were lifted up on a cloud and caught away from the places where they were preaching and set down before the door of the house wherein Mary dwelt. And they greeted each other and marvelled, saying: What is the cause wherefore the Lord hath gathered us together here?

[*In another text is this addition.* And Paul came with them

[195]

who was turned from the circumcision and taken with Barnabas to minister to the Gentiles. And when there arose among them a godly contention, which of them should first pray the Lord to show them the cause *of their coming,* and Peter exhorted Paul to pray first, Paul answered, saying: That is thine office, to begin first, since thou wast chosen of God to be a pillar of the church, and thou art before all in the apostleship: but me it befits not at all, for I am the least of all you, and Christ was seen of me as of one born out of due time, neither presume I to even myself with you; yet by the grace of God I am what I am.]

VI. Then all the apostles rejoicing with one mind finished their prayer: and when they had said Amen, lo, suddenly the blessed John came and showed them all these things. And the apostles entered the house and found Mary and saluted her, saying: Blessed be thou of the Lord which made heaven and earth. And she said to them: Peace be unto you my most beloved brethren. How came ye hither? And they told her how they had come, each one of them being lifted up on a cloud by the Spirit and set down in that place. And she said to them: God hath not deprived me of the sight of you. Behold I go the way of all the earth, and I doubt not that the Lord hath now brought you hither to give me comfort in the anguish that is to come upon me. Now therefore I beseech you that we all keep watch together without ceasing, until the hour when the Lord shall come and I shall depart out of the body.

VII. And as they sat about her comforting her, and for three days gave themselves to the praises of God, lo, on the third day, about the third hour of the day, sleep fell upon all that were in that house, and no man at all could keep waking save only the apostles and three virgins that were there. And behold, suddenly the Lord Jesus Christ came with a great multitude of angels, and a great light came down upon that place, and the angels were singing hymns and praising the Lord. Then the Saviour spake, saying: Come, thou most precious pearl, enter into the treasury (receptacle) of eternal life.

VIII. Then Mary fell on her face on the pavement, worshipping God, and said: Blessed be the name of thy glory, O Lord my God, who hast vouchsafed to choose me thy handmaid and to commit to me thy secret mystery. Remember me, therefore, O king of glory; for thou knowest that with all my heart I have loved thee and have kept the treasure committed unto me. Receive me therefore thy servant and deliver me from the power of darkness, and let not any assault of Satan meet me, neither let me see ugly spirits coming to meet me. 2 And the Saviour answered her: When I was sent by the Father and for the salvation of the world was hung on the cross, the prince of darkness came to me: but whereas he prevailed not to find in me any sign of his work, he departed vanquished and trodden down. Thou when thou seest him shalt see him indeed according to the law of mankind whereby the end, even death, is allotted thee: but he cannot hurt thee, for I am with thee to help thee. Come thou without fear, for the heavenly host awaiteth thee to bring thee into the joy of paradise. 3 And as the Lord thus spake, Mary arose from the pavement and laid herself on her bed, and giving thanks to God she gave up the ghost. But the apostles saw her soul, that it was of such whiteness that no tongue of mortal men can worthily express it; for it excelled all whiteness of snow and of all metal and silver that glistereth with great brightness of light.

IX. Then the Saviour spake, saying: Arise, Peter, and take

[197]

the body of Mary and bear it unto the right-hand side of the city toward the east, and thou wilt find there a new sepulchre where ye shall place it, and wait till I come unto you.

2 And when the Lord had so said, he delivered the soul of the holy Mary to Michael which was set over paradise and *is* the prince of the people of the Jews: and Gabriel went with them. And immediately the Saviour was received up into heaven with the angels.

X. Now the three virgins that were there and watched took the body of the blessed Mary to wash it after the custom of burials. And when they had stripped it of its apparel, that holy body shone with such brightness that it could indeed be touched to do the service thereof, but the appearance could not be looked upon for the exceeding flashing of light: and a great splendour appeared in it, and nothing was perceived by the sense when the body was washed, but it was most pure and not stained with any manner of defilement. And the body of the blessed Mary was like the flowers of the lily, and a great sweetness of fragrance issued from it, so that nothing like that sweetness could elsewhere be found.

XI. Then therefore the apostles laid the holy body upon a bier and said one to another: Who shall bear the palm before her bier? Then John said to Peter: "Thou who art before us in the apostleship oughtest to bear this palm before her bed. And Peter answered him: Thou only of us art a virgin chosen of the Lord, and hast found such favour that thou didst lie on his breast: and he when he hung for our salvation on the tree of the cross committed her unto thee with his own mouth. Thou therefore oughtest to carry this palm; and let us take up the body to bear it unto the place of the sepulchre. 2 Thereafter Peter lifted up the head of the body

and began to sing, saying: Israel is come out of Egypt. Alle-
luia. And with him the other apostles bore the body of the
blessed Mary, and John carried the palm of light before the
bier. And the rest of the apostles sang with exceeding sweet
voices.

XII. And behold a new miracle. There appeared a very
great cloud over the bier like the great circle that useth to be
seen about the splendour of the moon: and an host of angels
was in the cloud sending forth a song of sweetness, and the
earth resounded with the noise of that great melody. Then
the people came out of the city, about fifteen thousand, and
marvelled and said: What is this sound of such sweetness?
2 Then there stood one and told them: Mary is gone out of
the body, and the disciples of Jesus are singing praises about
her. And they looked and saw the bier crowned with great
glory and the apostles singing with a loud voice. And behold,
one of them who was a prince of the priests of the Jews in his
degree was filled with fury and wrath and said to the rest:
Behold the tabernacle of him that hath troubled us and all of
our nation, what glory it hath received. And he came near
and would have overthrown the bier and cast the body on the
earth. And forthwith his hands dried up from his elbows and
clave to the bier. And when the apostles lifted the bier, part
of him was hanging and part clave to the bier, and he was
wrung with extreme torment as the apostles went on and
sang. But the angels that were in the clouds smote the people
with blindness.

XIII. Then that prince cried out, saying: I beseech thee,
holy Peter, despise me not in this so great necessity, for I am
sore tormented with great pains. Remember that when the
damsel that kept the door knew thee in the judgement hall
and told the rest, that they might challenge thee, then I spake

good on thy behalf. Then Peter answered and said: It is not mine to give thee ought: but if thou believest with thy whole heart on the Lord Jesus Christ, whom this woman bare in her womb and continued a virgin after the birth, the mercy of the Lord, which by his great pity saveth the unworthy, shall give thee healing.

2 Whereunto he answered: Do we not believe? but what shall we do? The enemy of mankind hath blinded our hearts, and shame hath covered our faces that we should not confess the mighty works of God; especially when we did curse ourselves, crying out against Christ: His blood be on us and on our children. Then said Peter: See, that curse will hurt him that continueth unbelieving in him, but unto them that turn to God mercy is not denied. And he said: I believe all that thou sayest to me: only I beseech thee, have mercy on me lest I die.

XIV. Then Peter made the bier stand still and said to him: If thou believest with thy whole heart in Jesus Christ, thine hands shall be loosed from the bier. And when he had so said, straightway his hands were loosed from the bier and he began to stand on his feet: but his arms were yet withered, neither did the pain depart from him. 2 Then Peter said to him: Go near to the body and kiss the bed and say: I believe in God and in the Son of God whom this woman bare, even Jesus Christ, and I believe all things whatsoever Peter the apostle of God hath told me. And he came near and kissed the bed, and forthwith all pain left him and his hands were made whole. 3 Then began he to bless God greatly and to speak out of the books of Moses testimonies unto the praise of Christ, so that even the apostles themselves marvelled and wept for gladness, praising the name of the Lord.

XV. But Peter said to him: Take this palm at the hand

of our brother John, and go into the city and thou wilt find much people blinded; and declare unto them the mighty works of God, and whosoever believeth on the Lord Jesus Christ, lay this palm upon their eyes and they shall see: but whoso believe not shall continue blind. 2 And when he had so done, he found much people blinded and lamenting thus: Woe unto us, for we are become like the men of Sodom that were stricken with blindness. Nothing remaineth for us now save to perish. But when they had heard the words that the prince spake which was healed, they believed on the Lord Jesus Christ, and when he laid the palm upon their eyes, they recovered sight; but whoso of them continued in hardness of heart died. And the prince of the priests went forth to the apostles and gave back the palm and declared all that had come to pass.

XVI. But the apostles carrying Mary came into the place of the valley of Josaphat which the Lord had showed them, and laid her in a new tomb and shut the sepulchre. But they sat down at the door of the tomb as the Lord had charged them: and lo, suddenly the Lord Jesus Christ came with a great multitude of angels, and light flashing with great brightness, and said to the apostles: Peace be with you. And they answered and said: Let thy mercy, O Lord, be upon us, like as we have hoped in thee.

2 Then the Saviour spake unto them, saying: Before I ascended up unto my Father I promised you, saying, that ye which have followed me, in the regeneration when the Son of man shall sit on the throne of his majesty, ye also shall sit on twelve thrones, judging the twelve tribes of Israel. Now this woman did I choose out of the tribes of Israel by the commandment of my Father, to dwell in her. What then will ye that I do with her? 3 Then said Peter and the other

apostles: Lord, thou didst before choose this thine handmaid to become thine immaculate chamber, and us thy servants for thy ministry. All things didst thou foreknow before the worlds with thy Father, with whom to thee and the Holy Ghost there belongeth equal Godhead and infinite power. If therefore it might come to pass before the power of thy grace, it hath appeared right to us thy servants that, as thou having overcome death dost reign in glory, so thou shouldest raise up the body of thy mother and take her with thee rejoicing into heaven.

XVII. Then said the Saviour: Be it done according to your will. And he commanded Michael the archangel to bring the soul of the holy Mary. And behold, Michael the archangel rolled away the stone from the door of the sepulchre, and the Lord said: Rise up, my love and my kinswoman: thou that didst not suffer corruption by union of the flesh, shalt not suffer dissolution of the body in the sepulchre. 2 And immediately Mary rose up from the grave and blessed the Lord, and fell at the Lord's feet and worshipped him, saying: I am not able to render thee worthy thanks, O Lord, for thine innumerable benefits which thou hast vouchsafed to grant unto me thy handmaid. Let thy name be blessed for ever, redeemer of the world, thou God of Israel.

XVIII. And the Lord kissed her and departed, and delivered her to the angels to bear her into paradise. And he said to the apostles: Come near unto me; and when they had come near, he kissed them and said: Peace be unto you; as I have been always with you, so will I be even unto the end of the world.

2 And immediately when the Lord had so said he was lifted up in a cloud and received into heaven, and the angels with him, bearing the blessed Mary into the paradise of God.

But the apostles were taken up upon clouds and returned every one unto the lot of his preaching, declaring the mighty works of God and praising the Lord Jesus Christ, who liveth and reigneth with the Father and the Holy Ghost, in a perfect unity and in one substance of the Godhead, world without end. Amen.

7. EXTRACTS FROM THE ARABIAN BOOK OF THE PASSING OF THE MOST BLESSED VIRGIN MARY [1]

Some extracts from this apocryphon, which is more wordy in style than that attributed to Melito of Sardis, are given to round out the latter.

Chapter IV contains a very beautiful prayer of Our Lady to her Son on behalf of all mankind. The basic idea of Mary as the Mediatrix has rarely been expressed in so touching a fashion, even though the objects of the Virgin's supplication seem overly earthbound.

The disciples came forward, and they said to Mary: "Mother of Light, pray for the world which you are about to leave." And, with tearful voice, the blessed Mary said:

"O my Lord, my God, and my Master, Jesus Christ, at the will of the Father, in in strength of the Spirit, and by action of your own divinity and your own will, you did create the heavens and the earth and all that therein is. I beg you to hear the prayer I offer for your children reborn in baptism, for the just and for sinners. Grant them your grace. Receive all who gather together in your name, all who make offerings in your name, all who call upon you in prayer, in hope, and in suffering. Grant them a safe issue from their troubles, so

[1] Translated by A. G.

that they may grasp those things for which they have hoped in faith. Deliver them from threatening evils; heal them in illness; increase them in their estate; multiply their children; support them in all their worldly endeavors; and finally grant them the happiness of sharing in your kingdom. Cast out Satan their enemy, full of ill-will; strengthen them and lift them up into the flock ruled by the Good Shepherd, full of mercy and loving kindness. Grant the prayers, in this life and in the life to come, of all who ask your self in my name. May they be aided by your help, as you have promised; for you are mindful of what you have sworn to do; you are abundantly merciful; your name is worthy of all praise now, henceforth, and for evermore. Amen."

And the Lord said unto her: "What you have asked, that I do grant. At your prayer, I will not shut up my grace and my mercy."

All things created were filled with joy and cried out: "So be it."

A little further on in the same chapter, we find the account of Saint Thomas, a doubter of the Assumption of Mary as he had been of the Lord's Resurrection. Our Lady gives him her sash as proof. Medieval art often depicts this scene.

And the unspotted Virgin was triumphantly borne aloft in a chariot of light. Then a cloud covered all that stood about her. There remained only the disciples who persevered in prayer for three days during which they heard the continuous chanting of hymns of praise. While they were still together, behold Thomas, one of the disciples, cometh on a cloud just as the body of the most blessed Mary was being borne on high by the angels; and he called aloud to them to stop that he might be blessed by her.

Then when he came into the company of the other disciples who were continuing in prayer, Peter said to Thomas: "Thomas, our brother, what has delayed you from being present at the passing of the Mother of the Lord Jesus, and from seeing the great wonders which have been wrought in her honor? You have failed to receive her blessing."

And Thomas replied: "My duties in the Lord's service made it impossible for me to be with you. Yet the Holy Spirit has revealed to me all that has taken place while I was preaching the grace of Our Lord in the Indies, where I have baptized the king's nephew, Golodius. Now, tell me where you have placed the body of Our Lady."

They replied: "In this tomb." And he said: "I wish to see her and to be blessed by her. Then will I be able to affirm the truth of all that you have told me."

Then the disciples cried out: "Always are you distrustful of whatsoever we tell you. You are now doubting, just as you were when the Lord arose and until you were satisfied by being allowed to finger his wounds and to place your hand in his side. Only then did you say: 'My Lord and my God!'"

To this Thomas made response: "That I am Thomas, you know, I will not rest until I have seen the tomb wherein Mary was buried. Else I shall not believe."

Peter arose hastily and in anger, and with the help of the disciples he drew aside the stone of the tomb, and they all went within. They found the tomb empty, and they were greatly amazed and cried out: "While we were away the Jews have come and have taken the body to do what they will with it."

But Thomas said: "Be not fearful, O my brothers; for just

[205]

as I was borne here from the Indies on a cloud, I beheld the holy body surrounded by a great company of angels. She has gone up on high in triumph. Loudly did I beg that the Holy Mary would bless me and she gave me this sash."

Finally, Chapters V and VI of this Arabic apocryphon describe the glorification of the Holy Virgin in great detail, reporting also miracles wrought by her on earth and, in its peculiar fashion, showing the origins of devotion to Our Lady. Toward the end a prayer is put into the mouth of the Apostle John, again emphasizing the intercessory role of the Mother of God.

CHAPTER V

AFTER MARY HAD BEEN ASSUMED into heaven, the Lord Jesus Christ came to her, and with him a great company of the heavenly court. The pillars of heaven are set upon the earth, and its wall—from which there issue forth four rivers—reaches up aloft. In the time of the deluge that was upon the earth, the Lord did not allow the waters to reach Paradise.

Now Jesus said unto the blessed Mary: "Gaze upon the glory to which you have been raised."

She looked about and she saw greater glory than the eye of man can bear. And behold, Enoch, Elijah, Moses, and all the prophets and patriarchs, and the elect came and adored the Lord and the blessed Mary. And then they withdrew.

Thereafter the Lord said to Mary: "Behold all the good things I have prepared for the saints as I have promised." Lifting up her eyes, Mary saw bright and shining mansions; she saw the glorious crowns of the martyrs. She turned her eyes to the fragrant and lofty trees from which there went forth a perfume of which no one can tell.

The Lord plucked the fruit of these trees and gave them to the blessed Mary that she might eat of these beautiful and luscious fruits of Paradise. Then he said: "Go forth and behold the heights of heaven."

And she went aloft, and she saw the first and the second heaven. In the third heaven she beheld the heavenly mansion raised high above the earth; and she saw wondrous things. She praised God the creator in that he had done all sorts of wonderful works in the heavens, wonders which man cannot decry nor understand.

And the Lord bade the sun to stop at the gates of heaven, so that one side of it should tarry near Paradise. And the Lord sat above the sun in a chariot of light.

And the blessed Mary beheld all the treasures of light from which come snow, hail, rain, dew, lightning, and thunder, and all such things. She saw the throngs of flying angels who cried out: "Holy, holy, holy is the Lord of hosts." She saw the twelve great courts of the sun, and before each a guard set. And she saw the great gate of the heavenly Jerusalem upon which she rejoiced to behold inscribed the names of the Just, the names of Abraham, Isaac, Jacob, David, and all the prophets since the days of Adam.

Blessed Mary went in by the first door as the angels bowed down and praised her. Then, as she went in by the second door, the cherubim offered her their orisons, while when she came to the third door, it was the seraphim who offered her theirs. When she had paassed the fourth door, all the great company of the angels worshipped her; when she had passed the fifth door, lightning and thunder praised her; and when she had passed through the sixth door, all the angels cried aloud: "Holy, holy, holy is the Lord of hosts; Salvation and glory to you." When she entered the seventh door, the light

[207]

praised her; when she had passed the eighth door, rain and dew worshipped her. When she came to the ninth door, Gabriel and Michael, with other angels, fell down before her; at the tenth door, the sun and the moon, the stars and all the planets worshipped her; when she came to the eleventh door, the souls of the disciples, the prophets and the just praised and worshipped her. As she came through the twelfth door, she beheld her Son seated upon a bright throne and encompassed about by great light. She bowed before the majesty of the Father, the Son, and the Holy Spirit.

When she had gazed upon the heavenly Jerusalem, when she had seen its majestic beauty, then was her soul struck with wonder; she knew not what she saw; but the Lord clasped her hand and showed her all the hidden joys in the treasure house of the Holy Church. And he granted her to see and to hear many things which eye hath not seen nor ear heard, things, moreover, of which no tongue has sung, things which the mind of man cannot fathom. Nevertheless, all these things shall be given to the faithful at the last day, in that time of great joyfulness which shall be theirs for ever after.

Then when the blessed Mary turned to the Lord, the Saviour of all that is, he said to her: "This is the house of Enoch, it is here that he prays for all time. Amen."

CHAPTER VI

WHEN THE BLESSED MARY raised her head she saw a multitude of men who were moving about in countless dwellings of rest. The perfume of incense was set forth, the hymn of praise was heard; and the multitude beheld this splendor and they gave praise to God.

And the blessed Mary said: "My Lord and my Master, who are these men?" And he replied: "Here are the resting places

of the just; here is their dwelling place. The light shines to
show their glory in my sight. On the last day, they will arise
to enjoy these good things. Then will they know a greater
joy, a joy without end; for their souls will rejoin their
bodies."

Then the blessed Mary saw another place, a darksome
region, from which there arose much smoke and an odor
fetid as brimstone. Therein was burning a great fire in which
many men languished and cried out tearfully. And the
blessed Mary said: "My Lord and my God, who are these
people who dwell in darkness and suffer the torments of
fire?" And he answered: "This is the place of Gehenna, which
yawns for sinners. It is prepared for them, and there shall
they remain until the last day when their bodies and souls
shall again be reunited in order that they may suffer greatly.
Bitter is their anguish because they have not done penance
for their sins. For evermore will lasting remorse be their
portion, stinging like the worm which dies not nor sleeps.
They have spurned my word: they have despised my grace;
they have denied my God-head."

As the blessed Mary listened to the praise of the just she
felt great joy; but when she gazed upon the lot of sinners,
she was seized with sadness; and she besought the Lord to
take pity on sinners, begging him to deal kindly with them
inasmuch as man is a weak creature. And the Lord gave her
his word, that he would do so.

Then he took her hand and he led her into the holy and
glorious Paradise, into the company of all just and holy souls.

And now, behold, letters from various places were sent to
the disciples who were at Rome; and they were brought to
Peter and Paul and John. These letters inquired what had
happened to Mary. And for this reason therefore are these

miracles concerning Mary made known: so that men may realize that she has appeared to many trustworthy persons.

Some of the miracles are now set down.

Ninety-two ships were afloat on the sea, and they were beset by strong winds and waves. The sailors prayed to Mary; and after she had shown herself to them none of the ships was lost but all came safely into port.

Some travellers, taken unawares by robbers who wished to despoil them, called upon Mary. She appeared before them and left the robbers blinded as if by lightning. The travellers continued on their way; and they joyfully gave thanks to God.

A widow had an only son. He went out for water and fell into the well. His mother cried out and said: "O holy Mary! help me and save my son!" At once Our Lady appeared to her, and she drew up her son out of the well so that he was not drowned.

A man had been afflicted for sixteen years with a grave illness; and had spent a fortune on medicine without being cured. Taking up incense he cast it into the fire and said: "O holy Mary, Mother of our Saviour, look upon my misery and cure my sickness." All at once, Our Lady stood before him; she put her hand upon him, and he was cured of his illness. He praised God's name, and he gave thanks to the blessed Mary.

A great ship was tossed upon the sea, and all on board cried out, saying: "Have pity on us, O blessed Virgin!" She appeared to them and brought them safely into port.

A fierce beast emerged from a cavern and confronted two women who were on a journey. It rushed up to devour them; but they called upon Mary, crying, "Save us!" At once, the Blessed Virgin appeared to them and she struck the dragon upon his jaws with her hand. His head split asunder, and the women went on their way praising God.

A merchant had borrowed a thousand farthings in order to purchase goods; but he lost his purse whilst on his journey. He did not realize his loss until he had gone a great distance. Then he began to strike his face, to tear his hair, and to weep, until he bethought himself of calling upon Mary; and he said: "O Blessed Virgin, help me." She appeared to him and said: "Follow me and do not be distressed." He followed her as she led him to the place where his purse was. He picked it up joyfully, and he went about his business, praising Almighty God and giving glory to Our Lady.

When the disciples learned of all these wonders which had taken place at Rome and in other places, they gave thanks to God. They rejoiced greatly, and they made a record of the things done by Mary during her life and after her death, which occurred in the year 345 of the age of Alexander.

And there were a great many more wonders wrought in other places which have not been reported to us. If we knew of them all and were to write them down, a great many books would be needed to contain them.

And the disciples said: "We wish to keep her memory on three days in each year, for we know that the angels have joyfully celebrated feasts in her honor, because it is due to her that mankind will be saved." Therefore, in her commemoration, they established that on the second day after Christmas a feast be kept in her honor with the intention that the locusts hidden in the earth might be destroyed, that harvests might prosper, and that rulers might have Mary's protection and might be at peace, one with another.

They established the fifth day of the month of Aiar in her honor for the intention that insects might not spring forth from the earth to destroy the harvest, for this would lead to famine and to the death of men in God's anger. Therefore do men now come to the houses of prayer in order to bewail their sins and to pray that God will deliver them from these scourges.

Finally, they established a festival in her honor on the fifteenth day of the month of Ab, which is the day of her passing from this world, the day on which she wrought wonders, the day on which the fruits ripen on the trees.

And they ordained that when an offering was to be presented to the Lord, it should be brought to the Church in the evening in order that the priests might pray over it, and they declared: "We have established the manner in which those who have been baptized are to make offerings, so that it is unnecessary that we repeat them for those who believe neither in you nor in your holy Mother, Mary. In your goodness you have prepared rewards for those who do believe. Grant to us and to those of our flock who have given ear to your commandments, the joyful possession of all that you have prepared for your chosen ones, for those who are dear to you. Grant to us those good things which eye hath not seen nor ear heard of, those good things which it hath not entered into the mind of man to conceive. Receive our prayers for the whole flock that you see gathered round about us. Grant that not one of them be lost. Receive them all under your protection; and help them through the intercession of the blessed Mary and the prayers of all the saints. Amen."

And despite my own unworthiness, the blessed Mary revealed unto me, John, the preacher of the Lord, all those things which Jesus Christ had shown to her; and she said to me: "Keep all these sayings and add them to the books which you had already written before my going forth from this transitory world. Without doubt, you will be asked about these things; and all who see your writings will be filled with joy and will praise God's name as well as my own, even though I am not worthy. I would have you know that in the latter days men will be exposed to grief, to war, to famine, and to terror, by reason of the great number of sins which they have committed; and because of their want of love, many calamities shall befall the earth. Yet whoso despises himself in this world and trusts not in his own strength, he shall be saved. Likewise, who so thirsts for the good things of God, and who so deals with his fellow-men in love and in mercy, who so strives manfully to do good, fearing the wrath of the Creator. Many wonders will be seen in heaven and on earth. Then shall come the everlasting Son, born of the Father before time was; and on the last day when he shall come to Bethlehem, I fear that he will not find faith nor justice among men."

And blessed Mary called unto me: "My Son"; and I replied:

"O my Mother, may salvation attend you. May your blessing fall upon all to whom you turn your gaze. I trust in your prayers and in your intercession. Free the world from sorrow, and grant men to walk in paths of truth and justice. May God's love never be wanting to Adam and to the children of Adam; for they are creatures fashioned by the hand of the Lord. May the enemy of mankind be cast out from among them, by the Lord's mercy."

And the blessed Mary said, "Amen."

The number of the years during which the Virgin, the Mother of God, lived upon earth is fifty-nine. From her birth until her entry into the Temple, three years went by; in the Temple she remained for eleven years and three months. For nine months she carried the Lord Jesus in her womb, and then she spent thirty-three years with him while he lived upon the earth. After his ascension into heaven she lived on earth for eleven years. This makes up the number of fifty-nine years. We trustfully hope in her prayers to her dear Son that he will bring our souls to everlasting life. Amen.

BIBLIOGRAPHIC NOTE

DESPITE THE ENORMOUS MASS of Marian literature—by no means of equal importance—it is strikingly true that very few works actually seek to portray the Holy Virgin, to study her character, to depict her in the context of her own times. Even the basic work of Père Terrien, *La Mère de Dieu et la Mère des hommes* (Paris, 1899; 1902), which is a mine of wonderful texts, offers little in answer to such requirements. One is more or less reduced to the work of F. M. Willam, *La vie de Marie, Mère de Jésus* (translated from the German, Mulhouse and Tournai, 1938), and to another book which is unusual and is especially attractive because it shows great knowledge of the Hebrew background, *Miriam* (Paris, 1928), by Mélanie Marnas. This work is, however, limited to the early years of Our Lady's life.

The study of the Gospel sources can best be undertaken in connection with the fine introduction written by Père Lagrange to *L'Évangile selon Saint Luc* (Paris, 1921), and the following works, as well: J. Huby, *L'Évangile et les Évangiles* (Paris, 1940); E. Levesque, *Nos quatre évangiles* (Paris, 1917); L. Vaganay, *Introduction à la critique textuelle néo-testamentaire* (Paris, 1934).

For the study of the Apocrypha there are numerous works, despite the fact that there do not exist French versions which are, like the English versions, complete, up to date, and readily accessible. The *Dictionnaire des Apocryphes,* edited by the Abbé Migne in collaboration with S. Brunet (1856-58), is still very useful despite its age. Two volumes of *Evangiles aprocryphes* (Paris: Picard, 1914; 1924), edited by Hemmer and Lejay are directly concerned with Mary. The publishing house of Letouzey has undertaken to bring out a great collection of apocrypha. All their editions are published with notes and commentaries. Also useful are M. Lépin: *Évangiles canoniques et évangiles apocryphes* (Paris, 1907); J. Variot, *Les Évangiles apocryphes* (Paris, 1878); Le Hir, *Études bibliques,* tome II (Paris, 1869); É. Amann, *Le Protévangile de Jacques et ses remaniements latins* (Paris, 1910); and various works of Nicolas, Chaîne, and articles in the Vacant-Mangenot *Dictionnaire de théologie catholique,* to mention only books written in French. As far as concerns the influence exercised by apocryphal texts, it is manifested in the various works of art to which reference is made in the present study, and in many books having to do with the history of literature; e.g., Bédier and Hazard, *La littérature française;* Gustave Cohen: *Le Théâtre en France au Moyen Age* (Paris, 1928); and in studies by A. Jeanroy, G. Duriez, Gaston Paris, as well as in works concerned with *The Golden Legend* and other medieval writings.

In order to trace the evolution of Christian conceptions of Mary, the student must turn to the major works in the field of Patristics. Certainly the most useful and the most readily available is F. Cayré: *Manual of Patrology and History of Theology,* (Paris, Desclée & Co., 1936), in which the article devoted to Mary provides details about the far-reaching doctrinal effects of these conceptions as well as full bibliographies of sources. *L'Histoire du dogme catholique* by René Draguet (Paris, 1946), is a noteworthy study which conveys excellently the fundamental workings of Catholic speculative thought concerning the understanding and development of dictrine, and an article by the same author in the handbook, *Apologétique,* of Brillant and Nédoncelle (Paris, 1937), sets forth the underlying theoretical presuppositions of the process. On this theme the famous work of Cardinal Newman, *An Essay on the Development of Christian Doctrine* (London, 1878; French translation, Paris, 1938), should be consulted, as well as the works of Tixeront, Marin-Sola and others.

On particular questions, the remarkable article by P. Pourrat in the *Révue apologétique* of 1934 (pp. 656-676), concerns the history and definition of the dogma of the Immaculate Conception. This is also the theme of the article of Le Bachelet in D'Alès: *Dictionnaire apologétique de la foi catholique;* tome III; cc. 209-275. There is a true *summa* on belief in Our Lady's Assumption by Père Martin Jugie, *La Mort et l'Assomption de la Sainte Vierge* (Bibliotheca apostolica Vaticana, 1944). The brochure of Canon J. Coppens: *La définibilité de l'Assomption* (Bruges, 1947), which is less searching but marked by wonderful clarity, should also be consulted.

There are far too many works on doctrine and devotion to permit any feasible attempt to list them all. Père Pie Régamey has gathered together a moving collection of *Les plus beaux textes sur la Vierge Marie* (Paris, 1942); A. Molien presents the best texts of the French School in his *Les grandeurs de Marie* (Paris, 1934). P. E. Neubert provides a simple but sound explanation of doctrine in his *Marie dans le dogme* (Paris, new ed., 1945). There are, however, a vast number of other works, among them books by P. Bernard, P. de La Brosse, P. Morineau and other writers; scarcely a month goes by without the appearance of another book.

[217]

Cardinal Newman's study, *Devotion to Our Lady in the Catholic Church* (published in a French translation, Paris, 1908), retains even today the authoritative value it has always had.

To conclude with a reference to Our Lady in art, it must be remarked that any bibliography would run to enormous length. No study of art can afford to ignore her: she is a leading figure in the masterpieces of Émile Mâle on Medieval art; Maurice Vloberg has devoted three magnificently illustrated volumes to her in *La Vierge et l'Enfant dans l'art français,* and *La Vierge notre Médiatrice* (Grenoble, 1939). And many others should be referred to, as well; e.g., Cécile Jéglot, Henri Ghéon, Abbé Broussole, Louis Réau, Louis Bréhier. In *La nouvelle révue théologique* (May-June and October, 1946), there are two articles by P. Duhr which provide valuable information.

TRANSLATOR'S NOTE

THERE IS A DISTINCTION BETWEEN the Continental usage of the term *Apocrypha* as M. Daniel-Rops uses it and that current in English and American circles, a distinction upon which it is perhaps well to insist if we are to understand exactly what these apocryphal sources are and exactly what is their value.

Perhaps no writer of our own day has expressed this distinction with greater lucidity than the late Provost of Eton, who wrote in the preface to his own splendid collection of apocryphal literature:

The words apocrypha and apocryphal, particularly the latter, have come to mean, oftener than not, in common speech, that which is spurious or untrue. They do not mean that in themselves, nor did they in the minds of those who first applied them to books. They began by being terms of dignity and respect: they have degenerated into terms of something like abuse. An apocryphal book was—originally—one too sacred and *secret* to be in everyone's hands: it must be reserved for the initiate, the inner circle of believers. But, in order to enlist respect, such books were almost always issued under venerable names which they had no true right to bear. We hear of apocryphal books of Adam, Moses, and so forth. The pretense was that these had lately been brought to light, after ages of concealment by pious disciples. I do not intend to write a history of the gradual degradation of the words: I need only say that the falsity of the attribution was soon recognized: and so (to pass over three centuries of transition), in the parlance of Jerome, who has influenced posterity more than any one else in this matter, apocryphal means spurious, false, to be rejected and, probably, disliked.

The application of the word Apocrypha to that Appendix to the Old Testament which we have in our Bibles is a new departure, due to the reformers of the sixteenth century, and it is not consistent either with the original sense of the word or with Jerome's usage of it, for that Appendix contains no books of secret lore (unless 2 Esdras be so reckoned), but several books which are not spurious, besides some that are. There is, then, some confusion here, and the existence of that confusion has led scholars in recent years to use the long word, pseudepigraphic (= falsely entitled) when they wish to describe a really spurious book, as distinct from those contained in our 'Apocrypha.' [1]

I am greatly indebted to a number of my friends and colleagues who have been good enough to read portions of this translation of M. Daniel-Rops' *Les Evangiles de la Vierge,* and who have made valuable suggestions to me: they must not, however, be held responsible for any errors which may be uncovered; for I have not, in every instance, adopted the suggestions which they made. I wish most cordially to thank Professor Veré L. Rubel, of the Department of English, Hunter College of the City of New York; Dr. Rosemarie Daele, Chairman of the Department of Modern Languages in Hunter College High School and Professor at the French University in New York; the Rev. Professor Austin Vaughan, S.T.D., of the Faculty of Saint Joseph's Seminary, Dunwoodie, New York; Mr. Clark Mills McBurney, Public Relations Director at Hunter College; Dr. Joseph H. McMahon, formerly of the Université de Paris; Mlle. Mariette Pinchart;

[1] Montague Rhodes James: *The Apocryphal New Testament* (© Oxford: at the Clarendon Press, 1924); pp. xiii-xiv.

and one of my former students, Mr. Harvey Fenster, all of whom allowed me to trespass on their time and knowledge. I am also grateful to Mr. Helmut Ripperger for helpful advice, and to the Librarian and Staff of the General Theological Seminary, particularly to Mr. Thomas, Acting Librarian in the summer of 1959, for the loan of books otherwise inaccessible to me. Miss Margaret Grant Plumb, Associate Librarian of Hunter College, was also most helpful in securing some needed reference material; and I have to thank Mr. Frank Giella of the Hunter College Duplicating Office for assistance in the reproduction of quoted passages in the second part of this book.

To the Clarendon Press, Oxford, I offer thanks on my own part, as well as on behalf of the author and the publishers, for permission to reproduce herein, passages from their publication, *The Apocryphal New Testament*, translated and edited by Dr. Montague Rhodes James, © Clarendon Press, Oxford.

The color illustrations are used by permission of Barton-Cotton Inc. of Baltimore, Md.

—ALASTAIR GUINAN

* * *

Scripture quotations throughout are from THE HOLY BIBLE IN THE ST. PETER'S EDITION (WESTMINSTER VERSION), *published by Hawthorn Books, Inc., New York.*

THE AUTHOR AND HIS BOOK

HENRI DANIEL-ROPS *is the nom de plume of Henri Jules Charles Petiot, born January 19, 1901, in France. The grandson of peasants and the son of an artillery officer, the young student majored simultaneously in law, geography and history, winning the equivalent of a Master's degree in each subject before he was 21 years old. Within a year he was teaching history as an associate professor, which he continued until 1945 when he retired as Professor of History at Neuilly. His nom de plume was adopted for his first book, a volume of essays published in 1926. He has used it since for his more than seventy books which include novels, historical studies, poetry, and children's books. His writings have brought him many honors, including election to the Académie Française in 1955, its youngest member. Other orders include Commander of the Order Saint Gregory the Great, and The Grand Cross of that order; Commander of the Order of Christ; and Knight of the Legion of Honor. He is also winner of the Académie Française Grand Prix. His greatest successes in this country have been* This is the Mass *and* Jesus and His Times. *Currently, he is acting as editor-in-chief of* The Twentieth Century Encyclopedia of Catholicism, *and has contributed one volume to the series as well as supervising the entire 150-volume work. He is a regular contributor to many French magazines and newspapers and edits a popular monthly magazine,* Ecclesia, *as well as publishing an intellectual quarterly. His published works in English are:* Misted Mirror *(Knopf, 1931);* Two Men and Me *(Rockwell, 1931);* The Poor and Ourselves *(Burns Oates & Washbourne, 1938);* Flaming Sword *(Cassell, 1941);* Death, Where is Thy Victory? *(Cassell, 1946);* Sacred History *(Longmans, Green,*

[223]

1949); Where Angels Pass (Cassell, 1950); St. Paul: Apostle of Nations *(Fides, 1953);* Jesus and His Times *(Dutton, 1954);* Book of Books *(Kenedy, 1956);* Book of Life *(Kenedy, 1956);* Cathedral and Crusade *(Dutton, 1957);* This is the Mass *(Hawthorn, 1958);* What is the Bible? *(part of* The Twentieth Century Encyclopedia of Catholicism*), (Hawthorn, 1958); and* The Heroes of God *(Hawthorn, 1959).*

THE BOOK OF MARY *(Hawthorn, 1960) was designed by Sidney Feinberg and completely manufactured by American Book–Stratford Press, New York City, except for the color inserts, which were printed by lithography by Barton-Cotton, Inc., of Baltimore, Md. The body type was set on the Linotype in Baskerville, a modern reproduction of the types cut in 1760 by John Baskerville of Birmingham, England, reflecting the style of stone inscriptions.*

A HAWTHORN BOOK

[224]